The Philippines

THE PHILIPPINES

JOHN COCKCROFT

ANGUS AND ROBERTSON

Contents

Acknowledgements

The author would like to thank Mariano Ezpeleta, Ambassador for the Philippines, Canberra, Gregorio Araneta II, Commissioner for Tourism in the Philippines, Minister Guillermo Sison of the Department of Foreign Affairs, and the Philippine Government. He is grateful also to Jacobo Clave, Press Secretary, and Dave Bakirin, Malacañang; Father Tom Larkin, Ateneo University, and Imelda Relucio, Quezon City; Jose Reyes, Gabine A. De Lee and Mr and Mrs Araneta, Makati; Hadji Aida B. Nuni, Hadji Jaimiddin Nuni, and A. Veloso, Zamboanga; Thomas Alhambra, Administrative Officer, Manila Zoological Gardens; Benny Farolan, Sita World Travel; Mr and Mrs J. Mapa, Maria Regina Mapa, Ana Victoria Mapa, Eddie Jose Manuel Rodriguez, Ben Cabera, Pontenciano Badillo, Isacio R. Rodriguez, Prior of the San Agustin Church, of Manila; Eric Casiño, National Museum of the Philippines; V. Veloso, Philippine National Airways; B. Marks, QANTAS Airways; Augusto Resurreccion, Board of Travel and Tourist Industry; Artemio Sianson, Chief of Statistics Section, Board of Travel and Tourist Industry; Salvador Peña, Executive Director, Jose Sarmiento, Staff Photographer, Hilario Francia, Chief of Promotions and Research, Lydia Aunario, Promotions and Research, of the Philippines Travel and Tourist Association; and others who assisted in the preparation of this book.

*Text and photographs
by John Cockcroft
Drawings
by Faye Owner*

First published in 1968 by

ANGUS & ROBERTSON LTD
221 George Street, Sydney
54 Bartholomew Close, London
107 Elizabeth Street, Melbourne

NATIONAL LIBRARY OF AUSTRALIA
REGISTRY NUMBER AUS 68-1171
SBN 207 95077 6

MANILA, THE GATEWAY

Manila, the main port of entry to the Philippines, is a city full of life. I was impressed on my recent journey there by the courtesy and friendliness of the Filipinos, the fragile beauty of the women, and the young people with their eager search for knowledge—such as the girl in a store reading a book *Western Thoughts*.

Oblivious to the blaring horns of other vehicles, a water cart nonchalantly crept along Roxas Boulevard during peak hour, watering the garden plots on the median strip. Urchins plagued the crowds on the sidewalks, begging for five centavos. These children were dirty, but their skins were in perfect condition and their bodies firm and well-rounded.

I also encountered, with mixed feelings, the sellers of *balut*. Filipinos consider *balut* (a boiled, partly-incubated duck egg) a delicacy. In Rizal province, ducks are raised solely for making *balut*. The unborn duckling, surrounded by a thin, brownish fluid, is eaten feathers and all.

I saw students going home from college and night school at nine o'clock; the staid and serious businessmen from overseas, whose personalities completely reversed in the nightclubs; the nightclubs themselves, and cocktail lounges in Mabini, where fifteen-year-old girls act as hostesses; and the cockfights, scenes of noise and confusion as people tried to place their bets.

Busy streets, the pearl and lottery-ticket sellers; the pickpockets, some whose amateurish efforts are easily noticed; the families at Luneta Park on a Sunday; the bizarre jeepneys and the smell of burnt gasolene that hangs heavily on the hot air of Manila; and the magnificent buildings of the new commercial centre at Makati—all these things reflect the many facets of life in Manila.

THE CITY OF MANILA

The Hotel Filipinas, where I stayed, has a roof garden overlooking Manila. From here you have an excellent view of the world-famous sunsets over Manila Bay. Roxas Boulevard, stretching to the right and left of the hotel, is the main outlet for traffic, and a common sight at dusk is the traffic congestion as cars travel home after the day's work. Horns blow incessantly; cars cut in and out. People stand near the embankment watching the activities in Manila Bay. Others wait for buses and jeepneys, or are busy watching for taxis. Over the noise of people and traffic a loud voice is heard, calling through an amplifier "Taxi, taxi!" This is a doorman at the hotel getting a taxi for one of the guests. Dusk is a bad time for travelling by taxi; it is almost impossible to hire one.

Across the huge expanse of Manila Bay you can see the far coastline. At the end of Roxas Boulevard fishermen prepare for work. These men go out at night, and come back in the early morning to dispose of their catch. A small market at the top of the boulevard sells freshly-caught fish brought in by the boats. In the harbour many oversea ships anchor in mid-stream. Some wait their turn to berth at the wharves—others are unloaded by lighters. When I was there, 16 vessels waited to unload, and four were being discharged by lighters. The wharves held only nine ships. Port facilities are inadequate for the volume of sea-going traffic coming in and out of Manila.

Across from the QANTAS building near the hotel stands the impressive United States Embassy. In an excellent position right on the waterfront, the embassy has large grounds and a heliport, used by helicopters from United States bases in the Philippines.

Outside the embassy, pedlars sell various wares. At Christmas time they sell hand-made paper stars, intricately fashioned from paper and tinsel, in colours of gold, blue, white, yellow and red, with gold and silver tinsel. From time to time a double-decker bus passes along the boulevard, on a sight-seeing tour.

Looking down at the crowds from the hotel roof, you notice little girls trying to sell newspapers, the inevitable street urchins begging for money, and the shoeshine boys carefully inspecting the shoes of passers-by in search of likely customers. The newspaper sellers' voices drift up to you, pleading "Buy my newspaper, Sir. Please buy my newspaper"—in such a plaintive way that you feel sorry if you already have one.

In the park that borders the bay, housemaids exercise dogs—kept by many householders as a means of protection. Some property owners employ security guards, behind high-walled fences that shield the house from the eyes of passers-by. Even in convents and schools security guards are commonplace, always well armed, some carrying revolvers and others automatic rifles.

The large Luneta Park, with its monument to Rizal, provides pleasure for many people of Manila. After work they walk through the park or sit and read the paper. Many visit the Chinese Gardens. A public address system plays contemporary music, and occasionally announces lost children. On a Sunday the park assumes a colourful, gay atmosphere. This is the best time to see it. Thousands come to have lunch there before returning home to prepare for the next week's work.

Manila, Makati and Quezon City reflect the rapid progress of the Philippines. New buildings are being erected, people hurry about their business, traffic is brisk, and the whole atmosphere is one of drive and industriousness. The new buildings are of steel, cement, and Philippine marble. In Manila, the Philam-life building allows visitors to go inside and look around. It is spacious and well constructed. At Makati visitors can travel to the roof of some new buildings, and the photographer has an excellent opportunity to record the city of Manila on film. Makati looks new—and is new, with startling modern architecture, wide, tree-lined streets, and very clean, pleasant surroundings. The new buildings at Quezon City also give an impression of rapid national growth—their architects trained in many parts of the world.

Traffic in Manila seems continuous—Roxas Boulevard is used all day and all night. Though the volume of traffic decreases shortly after midnight, it builds up again in the early hours of the morning. Thousands and thousands of cars pass over this road every day and night of the week. The colourful jeepney buses dominate this traffic.

Manila welcomes visitors, and travel agencies try to employ people who will give travellers only the best of service. The Y.W.C.A., which runs many courses for girls, has just begun a new project to train competent tour guides for the Philippines. One night Benny Farolan, from Sita World Travel, took

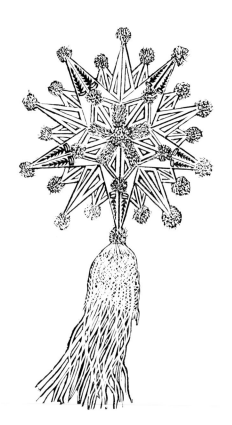

Tinsel Christmas star

me to the Y.W.C.A., to watch some of these girls graduate. I was impressed by the voluntary work put into this organization by the women of Manila.

Some of the night life: I was eager to see something of Manila at night, so later on the same evening Benny Farolan and I went to a Spanish cocktail lounge, drawn by the exciting beat of Flamenco music. As we went in some bar-girls standing outside the entrance of the place next door tried to catch our attention, and looked disappointed when we continued on our way. I had heard of these bar-girls, and wanted to learn more about their work. We stayed a short while at the Spanish lounge, then left and crossed the street to where some girls were sitting on chairs outside the nightclubs and bars, asking people to come in for a drink. We went into one of these places, and had no sooner found a spot to sit when two hostesses came over to join us at the table. One was 15 years old, and the other about 16.

Talking to these girls, I found that they start work about 7.00 p.m., and must stay in the bar until it closes—which may be 3.00 a.m. or later, depending on the number of drinkers. Their work is mainly to encourage customers to drink as much as possible—and also buy drinks for the girls, who receive a percentage of the cost of these drinks as wages. We ordered beer, but they wanted rum, explaining that they were expected to order the expensive drinks. Very business-like, they quickly finished their rum (which is actually a non-intoxicating kola), and clapped their hands, bringing a waiter to the table in a flash with more drinks. The girls' drinks, for which we had to pay a high price, would have barely filled two egg-cups.

The Philippines makes an excellent rum, called Tanduay, which is matured for five years, and sells in the shops for about U.S.$1.20. If you buy this in a hotel, you pay an exhorbitant price—two drinks bought at a hotel cost as much as a whole bottle bought at a store. At reasonable prices a lot more people would buy this locally-made rum; it is colourless, and equal to most of the internationally advertised rums.

The girls with us said that if they liked the person they were drinking with they were not averse to going home with him for the evening, after the bar closed. They could not understand at first that all we were interested in were the details of the hostess profession. When they accepted this, they were eager to chat about themselves, and one small bottle of beer was all we needed to buy. They seemed to ignore the worried looks cast from the bar, and when we asked why they did this sort of work, they said that the job was easy, and they could make much more money than other girls could by, say, working in a store. They gave us the very common story that they needed a lot of money so that they and their brothers could afford a good education.

We let the girls find more profitable company and left shortly after this conversation. The bar had been dimly lit, and it took a few minutes for our eyes to adjust to the bright lights of the street. We went to Tuboys at the end of the street, to be greeted again by hostesses. This time we drank alone. The pianist was playing in a style very similar to that of Eddie Duchin. I was surprised to notice that he was blind. His playing was superb, and he could play anything you mentioned. One of the hostesses sang—in a glorious voice, but decidedly off-key. We didn't stay long.

We then visited the most popular nightclub on the Roxas Boulevard—large, modern, brassy, and business-like. Here the hostesses are picked for their profession, and specially trained for some years. They are paid to entertain the visitor in a similar way to the geisha of Japan, usually receiving five pesos for introduction, ten pesos for every hour they spend with a guest, and 10% of the cost of all drinks bought by him. Again, they are not allowed to leave the club until the show is over for the night, which could be in the early hours of the morning. The hostesses are pretty, well dressed, and well versed in English and other languages. The average girl here makes about U.S.$20.00 a night—a high wage in the Philippines, enabling her to live in a well-furnished apartment.

As hostesses grow older, they tend to drift from one club to another, earning lower and lower salaries as the years go by, until they are no longer employed. Once they lose their looks, they have not much hope—too many young girls are seeking work of this kind.

The next night, we went to the Sulu restaurant at Makati. "*Sulu*" in Tagalog (a Philippine dialect) means "torch", symbolic of the fiesta, and denotes warmth and festivity. The restaurant has several dining rooms, each serving different kinds of food. We ate at the smorgasbord in the Rajah Room. Food was plentiful, varied, and excellently cooked, mainly in Filipino style. The diners are treated to an hour of folk dancing by a group of Filipino dancers. At the end of the show some are invited to participate in the Tinikling, a dance performed by jumping between two long pieces of bamboo—as the music becomes faster and faster. They often have great difficulty keeping up with the professionals, but this is part of the entertainment.

Another attraction is the singing group that moves round the tables. These entertainers sing in whatever language those sitting at the tables speak. The whole evening's entertainment can be enjoyable, including the food (the meat served here, incidentally, is flown daily by QANTAS from Australia). The cost for the evening, for two people, is about U.S.$4.00.

On Friday evening of the same week we tried another restaurant—the Plaza at Makati. Here we had steak, and again our food was excellently prepared. I was impressed by the decor of the restaurant. The menus and many of the decorations were done in hand-tooled leather.

Week-end in Manila: I spent Saturday afternoon watching the Bayanihan dancers at the Women's University. These dancers have achieved world acclaim, and have represented the Philippines in a number of countries, such as Mexico, the United States, and Australia. The word "*bayanihan*" means "group work" or "getting together". It depicts the Filipino tradition of groups of people helping one another. Even when shifting a house, people band together, lift the house bodily, and carry it to its new site.

COLOUR

Walking in Luneta Park on a Sunday morning in Manila

Inside San Agustin Church in the walled city of Intramuros

The Hall of Heroes at Malacañang Palace, Manila

The balloon seller in Luneta Park, Manila

The dances are a weekly feature at the university and visitors may see them. The girls dress in the national costume of the Philippines, or of one of its 56 provinces. Some of the dresses are exquisite, and all suggest eighteenth century Spanish or Muslim styles. Most costumes have a full-length panelled skirt, worn with a blouse. This blouse has characteristic "butterfly" sleeves—very wide, and gathered to the shoulder so that the top of the sleeve stands off in a crisp point. A bright scarf, folded into a triangle, covers the back and shoulders. Jewellery consists of a gold filigree necklace, earrings, bracelet, and a comb called a tambourine.

Muslim girls wear tight-fitting jackets with narrow sleeves, over a tubular skirt. At times long, loose trousers are worn, with a type of shawl that drapes over the shoulders and falls to the knees.

The country women wear a simple, very practical costume, shorter in length and with short sleeves. They wear an apron over the frock. Shoes are usually wooden, but sometimes slippers are worn.

For one of the dances, the *Pandanggo Sa Ilaw*, or Dance of the Lights, each dancer has lighted oil lamps balanced on her head and on the back of her hands. When the dance is done by a number of people, it is spectacular. The *Kzodaratan*, another dance, of Muslim origin, depicts a very stately way of walking. It was first performed hundreds of years ago in Lanao, Mindanao, as preparation for an event at the royal court.

Also that afternoon I saw the romantic *Mazurka Alcamphor*, a dance similar to a minuet, of Spanish origin. The principal dancer waves a handkerchief perfumed with camphor.

Sunday morning I spent just walking around. I have always found that Sunday is the best day for taking pictures, because people are relaxed and friendly. You can move about at a more leisurely pace, and talk freely to them. In the Philippines Sunday is a day of worship, and thousands of people attend the many magnificent churches.

In the afternoon I went into the countryside round Manila. Here the rhythm of life is slower, but the farmers were working—planting, sowing, cultivating, harvesting—as part of their continual seasonal pattern. Each year new ideas are implemented to give better yields—of rice, sugar, coconuts, or pineapples; yet the basic everyday life of the farmer remains much the same. Here you can see the real heart of the Philippines, the workers busy in the open air, on many types of farms scattered throughout the archipelago—and country people always spare the time to talk.

The houses I saw in the countryside all had flower gardens, with bougainvillea draped over the entrances and windows—a contrast to some parts of urban Manila.

THE 7,107 ISLANDS

An old Filipino legend tells that the world at first consisted of nothing but sea and sky. The only living creature at this time was a lonely bird, flying year after year over the waves, with nowhere to land. Finally the bird grew bored with this existence, and longed for somewhere to rest his weary wings. He deliberately provoked an argument between the sea and the sky, and retired to a safe distance to see what would come of this battle.

The sea thrashed and churned, throwing huge, foaming waves at the sky—who growled and grumbled, sending thunder rumbling across the waves. As he became wetter and wetter, however, the sky began to retaliate more violently, first with blinding flashes of lightning, then by hurling great boulders and clods of earth at the sea. These built up until the first pieces of land began to appear above the waves. Soon the sea and sky quietened down and when all was still again, the wily bird thankfully set his feet on solid ground for the first time. These small areas of land, say the Filipinos, were the islands of the Philippines.

Certainly the Philippines did have violent beginnings. Some scientists believe that the formation of the Philippines began about 65 million years ago, when Borneo and the Philippines were one land mass, thrust up from the ocean depths by volcanic action. For centuries the area was twisted by earthquakes and volcanoes, alternately rising and sinking beneath the sea. In this convulsion, Borneo was torn away from Mindanao, Mindanao shook itself free of the Visayas, the Visayas from Luzon, and Luzon from Taiwan. Today the Babuyan and Batan islands separate Taiwan from Luzon, and the Sulu Archipelago separates Borneo from Mindanao.

THE PHILIPPINES TODAY

The land itself: The Philippine Archipelago lies between latitudes five degrees and fifteen degrees north of the Equator. The islands are volcanic, bounded on one side by the western edge of the Pacific Ocean, and on the other by the South China Sea. On the eastern side of the Philippines is the second deepest trench of water in the world; the depth of the Pacific Ocean at Cape Johnson is 35,000 feet.

The 7,107 main islands of the Republic spread over 1,000 miles from north to south, and 625 miles across the widest part from east to west. The islands share a total length of about 11,000 miles of coastline.

Luzon, at the top of the Philippines, is about 500 miles from Taiwan; Jolo, in the south, is about 150 miles from Borneo. The closest distance between Australia and the Philippines is about 1,250 miles. Neighbouring countries are Sabah (North Borneo), to the south, Thailand, Singapore and Malaya to the west, Taiwan and China to the north, and Japan to the north-east. The

14

Philippines has no "neighbours" to the east; the nearest country in this direction is Hawaii, thousands of miles away.

The total land area, nearly 115,000 square miles, is concentrated mainly on the islands of Luzon and Mindanao, and has an average population density of about 284 to the square mile. The eleven largest islands are Luzon, Mindanao, Samar, Leyte, Negros, Mindoro, Panay, Palawan, Cebu, Bohol, and Masbate. Most of the economic development takes place on these islands, with limited development on some of the smaller ones. The Republic includes over 6,500 tiny islets less than a square mile in area.

The Philippines has over 60 natural harbours, and hundreds of rivers and bays. Manila Bay, with an area of 770 square miles and 120 miles of foreshore, is the main port. The islands, being in a volcanic belt, are very mountainous, with a comparatively small area of lowland. The islands are subject to floods, typhoons, earthquakes, and volcanic eruptions. Some volcanoes of interest are Taal, the lowest volcano in the world, which has erupted more than twenty times since records were kept, the last time in early 1968; and Mt Mayon, recognized as the most perfectly-formed volcanic cone in the world, 8,000 feet high, which has erupted more than 30 times since first records were taken in 1615. The highest volcano in the Philippines is Mt Apo, 9,600 feet high, in Davao province, Mindanao. Slightly smaller is Mt Pulog, 8,481 feet, in northern Luzon. At least ten Philippine volcanoes are very active.

The main mountain ranges are the Cordillera Central, and the Sierra Madre, both running north to south, roughly parallel to the coastline of Luzon—the Cordillera Central on the western side, and Sierra Madre on the eastern side, enclose the Central Plains of Luzon. The mountainsides are scarred by many watersheds and gullies—the cause of many landslides in the wet season, resulting in chaos for transport.

Climate and weather: Weather in the Philippines, governed by the Asian monsoon seasons, is usually tropical with high humidity. Temperatures vary considerably in some areas, depending on the topography. In Manila, temperatures usually range from 68 to 94 degrees.

The hottest month is May, and the coldest, January. The average yearly rainfall for the Philippines is about 90 inches, but some areas receive less than 40 inches, and others more than 160 inches. The Philippines, being a tropical country, experiences very little seasonal temperature variation. In June, July, and August, atmospheric pressure is low over the Philippines area, and air moving from high pressure areas creates winds moving north, north-east, or east, called the winter monsoons. In December, January and February, when high pressure exists over the Philippines, winds move towards the south and south-west. The Philippines has a complex weather pattern. Eastern parts of the region receive their heaviest rainfall during the summer months, and western parts of the Philippines have heavy rain in the winter months. Though some parts of the Philippines have distinct wet and dry seasons, others seem to have a wet "season" all year round.

The Philippine region is hit by many typhoons each year, some inflicting severe damage on buildings and crops. Most typhoons start in the western Pacific, and move across the Philippines towards China, or at times change course and move back towards Japan. During the main typhoon season, from June to November, as many as 100 typhoons may reach the Philippines.

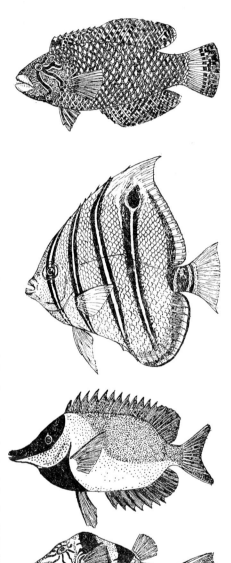

Colourful reef fish of Philippine waters —from top, Wrasse, Butterfly Fish, Fox-face, Toby

The strange bat-like Colugo

Land and vegetation: The mountainous areas of Luzon, in the northern Philippines, are mainly of sandstone and limestone. On Mindanao, in the south, the mountains are mainly of basalt. The Visayas have many different landforms, from mountain ranges to palm-fringed coral islands. On Bohol are the famous "chocolate hills"—unique perfectly-rounded hills, all about the same size, like a cluster of gigantic nodes on the surface of the earth.

The volcanic soils of the Philippines promote a rich, varied growth of plants. Most of the forests of the region, tropical evergreen rainforests, yield many kinds of commercial hardwood timbers. In the higher forests grow pines, and on the lower slopes bamboos, coconut palms and banyan trees. It is said that no other archipelago has as rich a variety of orchids and other plants as the Philippines. Over 10,000 species of plants have been recorded from the region. The national flower of the Philippines is the sampaguita—a small white blossom with a pleasant, lingering fragrance, made into garlands worn by Filipino girls and offered to visitors. Over 1,000 orchid species grow in the Philippines, and many of these are found nowhere else in the world.

The land animals: The Philippines has quite a few kinds of mammals, but no marsupials. Many of the animals show distinct specialization but their exact range is often uncertain. Animal life seems to be divided into two regions—the main islands; and the south-eastern islands of Palawan, the Calamian group (at the northern tip of Palawan), Basilan (at the south-eastern tip of Mindanao), and the Sulu Archipelago.

On the tiny island of Balabac, between Palawan and Borneo, a kind of chevrotain or "mouse deer" ranges—one of the smallest deer in the world. Axis deer found on Sulu were probably introduced a century or two ago. On the islands of Basilan, Mindanao, Leyte, Samar, and the Calamian group, red and brown deer occur, related to the sambar deer of Asia. Another deer, found on Masbate, Panay, and Guimaras (between Panay and Negros), and native to the Philippines, is dark-coloured with buff spots.

Wild water-buffalo, probably descended from domestic animals, can be seen in Luzon, Mindoro, the Calamian group, Masbate, Negros and Mindanao, but a very small buffalo, called the tamarau, on Mindoro, is native to the Philippines. This tiny buffalo, savage and untameable, often attacks and kills the larger water-buffalo, nearly twice its size.

Two kinds of wild pigs and a kind of monkey can be seen on most of the larger islands, and tiny primates called tarsiers are found from Basilan to Samar. Squirrels live on the eastern islands, and also on Palawan, and a strange anteater called the pangolin, on Palawan.

Carnivorous animals of the Philippines include shrews and otters, two kinds of civet cat, and a small wild-cat. Bats and flying foxes are very common, and another strange flying mammal is found in the Philippines—the colugo, which looks vaguely like a cross between a bat and a flying squirrel, and is sometimes called a "flying lemur".

Bird life in the Philippines is abundant—over 700 species have been recorded. Pheasants are confined to Palawan, but jungle fowl are found almost everywhere, and a strange megapode (or incubator bird) builds nest mounds in the warm ash on volcano slopes. Water and shore birds include snipe, plover, turnstone, herons, bitterns, and ducks. About 50 kinds of birds of prey live in the Philippines, ranging in size from a sparrow-sized falcon to the

16

large monkey-eating eagle—and twenty kinds of birds of prey are found no-where else in the world. Some twenty kinds of kingfishers, most of them native to the Philippines, live along the streams and waterways.

A dozen kinds of hornbills occur only in the Philippines. One kind of cockatoo and about twenty kinds of parrots and parrakeets live in the forests, as well as larks, barbets, broadbills, starlings, orioles, weaver finches, nut-hatches, titmice, shrikes, tailor birds, thrushes, flycatchers, swallows and swifts. The swift whose nest, collected for soup, is eaten with relish in Asian countries, lives in some parts of the Philippines.

About twenty kinds of woodpeckers, and the same numbers of cuckoos and honeyeaters are found here, and some twenty-eight species of colourful sun-birds. Some of the other kinds of birds in the Philippines are frogmouths, bee-birds, and night-hawks.

The Philippines has over 20,000 types of insects, including ants, termites, locusts, land-leeches, butterflies, moths, beetles, cockroaches, mosquitoes, and wasps. One of these wasps, the tiger hornet, is among the most feared of jungle creatures in the Philippines—just as terrifying as any of the venomous snakes of the region. Nesting in small colonies low to the ground, these large black insects have a four-inch wingspan, and a bright orange stripe across the abdomen. Occasionally they nest on a jungle path, where an unwary person might disturb them. One or two bites cause intense pain but, if the whole group of wasps attack, they can kill the strongest of men in a very short time.

Filipinos are very fond of honey, especially in places where sugar cane does not grow. Honey bees are encouraged to nest in trees with easy access.

Land and freshwater reptiles include many small lizards, such as skinks and geckoes, and large goannas, venemous snakes, the reticulated python and other pythons and boas, and the only sea-snake in the world known to have adapted itself to a life in fresh water (found in Lake Taal). Land turtles are also common, and a crocodile grows to a length of 25 feet, and may measure about three feet across the back.

About 40 kinds of frogs live in the Philippine region—most of them closely related to species found in Borneo. Scientists believe that these reached the islands on canoes laden with produce, or crossed many centuries ago when the Philippines region was connected to Borneo by land-bridges.

The sea animals: The seas on the western side of the Philippines and be-tween the islands, fairly shallow and warm, support a huge variety of marine creatures. Sea mammals are represented by dolphins, dugongs, and whales. The largest marine animal in these waters is the striped whale. Turtles, sea snakes, coral snakes, and the huge estuarine or sea-going crocodile are also common. Over 2,000 varieties of fish live in the Philippine region, including the smallest fish in the world, only half an inch long when fully grown. Most of the fish are of Indonesian origin, with some Chinese and Japanese kinds, and others similar to fish found near Tonga, Samoa, and Hawaii. Tereapon, catfish, perch, mudfish, mullet, milkfish, trevally, long-tom or garfish, shrimps, crabs, oysters and squid are caught close to shore by commercial fishermen. Salmon, herrings, and other fish are farmed in tidal pools. Oceanic fish are anchovy, bonito, sailfish, marlin, sharks, mackerel, barracuda, jewfish, bass, snapper, tuna, and many others. Many kinds of colourful reef shells come from the warm seas close to the islands.

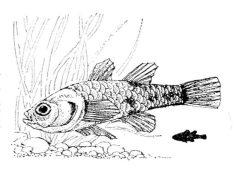

The smallest fish in the world (Pandaka pygmaea) drawn life-size in silhouette

17

THE FILIPINOS

The people of the Philippines separate by religion into three main groups. The majority are Christian—especially the lowland Filipinos who have known Spanish influence. The next largest group, the Muslims, belong to the southern islands such as Mindanao. Many people in the rugged, isolated areas of northern Luzon, and on Palawan, Panay, and Mindoro, still follow ancient religions that originated long before the Muslims and Spaniards reached the Philippines.

Traditional forms of painting, sculpture, writing, singing and dancing are still practised by the two groups of people unaffected by Christian teaching. Many of their implements, though classified as objects of art, were originally intended for practical use in work and war as well as for ornaments. The people from the mountain provinces have become world-renowned for their wood-carvings, sold in almost all the curio shops in Manila and elsewhere. Wood carving is also practised in Mindanao and in the Sulu Archipelago, but the main art medium here is brass. The Muslims, famous for their brassware, use this for many purposes in their daily life. They make knives and krises, with well-tempered blades, using bellows and forges to do their metalwork. The Muslims are also expert at inlay work—with intricate designs and placement of small inserts. Intricate detail is found in the delicate lacy decoration of the brassware. Both Muslims and mountain people excel in weaving cloth. Some people say that the techniques used in this work today are exactly the same as those used before the Spaniards came to the Philippines. This may be slightly exaggerated—some changes, some new ideas and new designs must have been adopted over a period of 400 years.

The Christian Filipinos have channelled their skills into different outlets, guided by the Spaniards and the Americans. Most of the magnificent statues in the churches were carved by Christian Filipinos.

BEFORE THE SPANIARDS CAME

The islands of the Philippines, Indonesia, Melanesia, Micronesia, and Polynesia are inhabited by (or contain small groups of) basically-related people, speaking languages of Malay-Polynesian origin. These people are often not only related by language, but also by customs and artifacts.

Some of the first people to settle in the Philippines could have been the ancestors of the present-day Polynesians. When Hindus arrived, about 4 B.C., they caused a general exodus of the Polynesians to the South Pacific, where they became firmly established.

Another migration brought people from Asia (either from the Gobi Desert in China or from the Himalaya Mountains) to the northern islands of the Philippines. These small, hardy people were the ancestors of the present-day

18

mountain tribes of northern Luzon—the Igorots, Bontocs, Ifugaos and Kalingas.

When the Chinese and the Arab traders visited the coasts of Luzon centuries ago, they found these tribes living on the shore. As foreigners began to settle in Luzon, the shy Igorots and other original tribes, reluctant to mix with these strangers, moved farther and farther inland, and high into the mountains, until they now live mainly in areas over 5,000 feet. One of the mountain tribes, the Ifugaos, built the spectacular rice terraces at Banawe some 3,000 years ago. Carved from the steep hillsides, these terraces rise layer after layer like huge broad staircases. If all the terraces were placed end to end they would stretch more than half way round the world.

Today the mountain tribes live in much the same way as they did thousands of years ago. Though they inhabit high, cold regions, the mountain people do not wear many clothes. Their only garment is usually a brief loincloth of finely hand-woven cotton, decorated with intricate, colourful designs. At home, they stay close to a fire for warmth, but outside they move actively to keep warm.

Once, many years ago, most of these mountain people were headhunters, and a small group of headhunters still lives in remote mountain areas of northern Luzon. These are a racial mixture of Igorot and Negrito—a small, wiry, dark-skinned people thought to have originated from the same migration as the New Guinea highlanders. Unlike other headhunting tribes, these people from the Bontoc area never ate any part of their victim's body—all they sought was the head trophy. Headhunting was the only way a man could earn a higher place in his society and, as no man was allowed to marry a girl of higher standing than himself, he had to collect several heads to prove himself worthy of such a wife.

Spirits once played an important part in the lives of all Filipinos, and many who have been converted to Christianity or the Muslim faith still hold a few of their ancient beliefs. Today, in some places, a person never throws hot or boiling water on the ground in case he injures a lurking spirit and so brings misfortune on himself or on his family. Ancestor worship, strongly adhered to by ancient Filipinos, may still be observed today, though merged with Catholicism. On All Saints' Day, many families place lighted joss sticks or candles on the graves of their dead.

The Igorots still worship their ancient gods. The highest of these, ruler of the other gods, is called the Diwata. Below him are lesser gods, the most important being the granary god. This god protects workers in the rice paddies, when they plant and harvest crops, and he also prevents the crop from being damaged by evil spirits. Idols of the granary god are small figures in a squatting position, about 18 inches to two feet tall. When the rice has been harvested the idol is taken from the field and placed inside the store-house where the harvested grain is kept, or just outside the door of the granary. The god ensures that the grain is not stolen, and frightens off any evil spirits.

Another god is the "sitting-down" god, or the father god, the second highest of all the gods. He is a household god, and his idols can only be owned by wealthy Igorots—usually the chief, and a few select nobles.

Other religious symbols, bamboo sticks, ward off evil spirits. In some of their dances, the Igorots make offerings to their gods. Other dances are tribal war dances, a carry-over from the days not so very long ago when few tribes were at peace, except when a chief's daughter of one tribe married the chief of another

Stone granary god

19

Delicate pattern of Muslim brassware

tribe or his son, thus uniting the two groups. The mountain people fought fiercely when their territory was encroached upon.

On Palawan Island live a group of people with light complexion and long hair. They exist in primitive fashion, and their food consists of local animals from the mountain areas and fish caught in the streams. Few others ever see or communicate with these people—not even the other dwellers of Palawan go near them. They are a ferocious race, prepared to go to any length to keep their privacy. Very little is known of their origins or ancestry—some people say that this tribe is one of the so-called "lost tribes of Israel"—but they have certainly been in the Philippines for a very long time, and have remained unaffected by the influences of Hindu, Muslim, or Christian religions.

The Muslims: In the fifteenth century the Faith of Islam, which had long been established in the Moluccas, began to spread to the southern islands of the Philippines, from the Sulu Archipelago to Mindanao. Eventually the Muslims reached the southern parts of Luzon. The people of Mindanao, who were once inveterate pirates and used to make periodic raids along the coasts of other Philippine islands, readily embraced the Muslim faith, since it gave them a spiritual reason for warfare against non-believers.

The Muslims belong to several groups, living in clans, tribes, settlements and provinces, from the coasts of Mindanao to the mountains round Lake Lanao, where they have dwelt for many years. Another group called the Magindanao, live on the island of Jolo (pronounced Holo) in the Sulu Archipelago. Some Muslims, called Sea Gypsies, live all their lives on boats, sailing between the Philippine islands.

The Spaniards later called all Muslims "Moros", because they reminded them of the Moors. This is actually a misnomer, and the Muslims themselves give the name "Moro" to a person who follows an ancient Filipino religion. The Muslims are a devout religious group, with a very colourful background. For many hundreds of years the people in the Lake Lanao area, 3,000 feet above sea-level, have built barricades round their villages so that no invaders can enter. They still adhere to their ancient Muslim practices, and their way of life has changed very little since the Muslim faith first came to the Philippines.

The Muslims fought the Spaniards for 300 years, and fought the Americans after that—they have never been conquered by any nation. General Pershing made a treaty with them permitting the Americans to stay in the Philippines, signed on the condition that the Americans did not bother the Muslims. The Americans, until the invention of the .45 pistol, could not effectively stop the Muslims in warfare. The .38 pistol caused only superficial wounds, for the Muslims, when they went to war, bound themselves with cloth in such a way that no matter where they were hit, they would not lose much blood. They still had freedom to move and fight, but the bindings provided a tourniquet for any wound they received.

The Muslims were fanatical in their belief that if they killed Christians it was easier for them to get to heaven. The more they killed, the quicker would be their passage. A Muslim sect called the Juromentado (pronounced Huromentado) presented themselves as sacrifices. They fasted for several weeks, meditating, then they shaved their hair and went on a rampage. They stabbed with their krises any Christians they met—until they themselves were killed. This

20

Lottery ticket seller on a street in Manila

21

Young girls of Manila

The Sulu restaurant at Makati, near Manila

*The entrance to the Philamlife building
in Manila*

*Makati, the modern business centre a
few miles from Manila*

Part of the modern district of Forbes Park, called "Millionaires' Row"

Luneta Park, Manila, where many families find quiet rest

*Housing is a problem in some parts of
the Philippines*

*A rural Filipino home, with thatched
roof of nipa palm*

Mount Mayon in southern Luzon,
a perfect 8,000 foot volcanic cone

Lake Taal, a volcano within a volcano

The crocodile, one of the Philippines'
dangerous reptiles, grows to a length
of 25 feet

A Muslim village in southern Mindanao

*A suspension bridge spanning a river
in Mindanao*

*Cottage in Zamboanga, where couples
live rent-free for their wedding holiday*

People of the Philippines show a great zest for life when young, a sophistication in their grown years, and wisdom and dignity with age . . .

38

A large fishing vessel from the Visayas

One of the many vintas used by the
Muslim people of Mindanao

Muslim women preparing food in
Mindanao

49

Muslim brassware, renowned for its design and craftsmanship

The candle seller outside Manila Cathedral

struck terror into the Christian Filipinos, and even today some people believe that the dreaded Juromentado are still active.

The social structure of the Muslims is a fascinating study. In each town a Sultan reigned as chief. Every town had a number of villages, each governed by a datu, or "prince". To attain power, and ensure strength and family unity, the sultan married one of his daughters to the strongest of the datus. The sultan was not appointed, but came from an ancient heritage of rulers—a royal family similar to those in Polynesia.

According to legend, Prince Hadramaputra was once brought to earth by a big bird, called Sarimanoc. This bird carried the prince to Lanao, which was infested with large dragons and snakes, making it a holy place. The dragons and snakes protected the area so that no one could enter. The prince, with the help of the bird, killed all the dragons and snakes and, when he had done this, found a princess living in the lake. She had been a captive of the snakes and dragons. The prince and princess married, and all their descendants became the sultans.

Sultans were graded in position—first, second, and so on. They held court with quite elaborate ceremony. The highest sultan had a gold throne, gold ornaments, a gold Sarimanoc replica, multi-coloured umbrellas, golden chests, and the most lavish setting imaginable. The second-degree sultan had all these objects made of silver, and pearls were his only precious jewels. A sultan held court for many reasons, such as when a foreigner visited his area, or when a question of marriage had to be decided.

Drums and brass gongs were often used in court—of different sizes and types, depending on the occasion. One drum, about 12 feet long, larger at one end than at the other, produced two distinct sounds. Called a *tabo*, this was used to summon people, and in the mosques to call people to prayer. Other drums found uses in various rituals and ceremonies, dancing, and celebrations. Different brass gongs, some quite large and about four feet in diameter, were struck in court to order silence, or to summon people, and other gongs for celebrations. A series of eight gongs, of varying sizes, each giving a separate sound and played like a piano, had a range of one octave.

The Muslims also played guitars, made to resemble boats or snakes. (Snakes are still revered by the Muslims as supernatural creatures, and a snake is believed to be the guardian of the tree of life in heaven.)

They had a kind of jewsharp, for serenading. The instrument was played in such a way that the girl could understand what was being sung by the boy, and she could answer, with her own jewsharp. This instrument could be especially handy when the boy was forbidden to enter the girl's house. Long musical conversations could be held in this way.

The clothing worn by the Muslims was all hand woven—even the patterns on materials were hand-embroidered by the women. The fabrics for the clothes of nobles were made from imported raw silk. Common people wore clothes of cotton, of cloth made from tree-bark, similar to tapa, or of cloth made from the fibres of a kind of banana plant, called abaca.

From the early days the Mindanao people lived as pirates and bandits, bringing back to their homes any gold, silver or jewels they found on their travels. The men captured in raids became Muslim slaves, sold by auction in a market place, or kept as part of a dowry by a Muslim intending to marry.

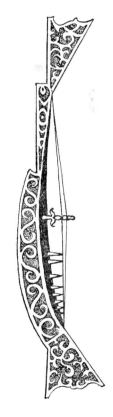

Muslim guitar-like instrument

The early sixteenth century: By the time Magellan came to the Philippines,

53

A candle offered at an altar

D

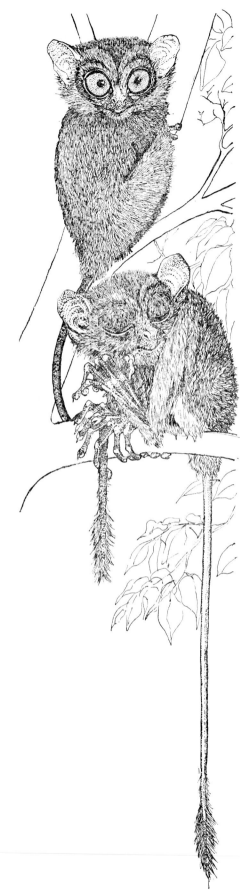

Philippine tarsiers

in 1521, the Filipino people had evolved a distinct culture of their own, influenced in many ways by contact with Hindus, Chinese and Arabs. The Hindus had reached the Philippines in about the fourth century before Christ, and their influence was especially felt on the islands of Mindanao, the Visayas, Palawan and Mindoro, where the people learned to communicate in old Sanskit writing. Folklore, metal-work, dress, and art also showed traces of Hindu life.

Trade with China began in about the 9th century. The Chinese merchants did not penetrate inland, but waited on the shore for the Filipinos to come down from the hills. In exchange for sandalwood and other goods, the Chinese gave the Filipinos glass beads, porcelain ware, and silks. Some of the jars and urns can be seen today, such as one that came to Mindanao in about 1200.

In 1275, an invasion force from Java penetrated the Philippines from the Sulu Archipelago up as far as Luzon. This force stayed in the islands for about 20 years before returning to Java. Other people came from Borneo to settle in the southern islands of the Philippines. By the middle of the 14th century, Cambodia and Indo China were also trading porcelain in the northern Philippines, and soon after this Annam, Siam, and Tonkin came to the Philippine shores.

All this brought changes to the Filipino way of life. By the 16th century, the Filipinos had their own alphabet, of either Indian or Arabic origin, and they wrote with sharp sticks or iron on pieces of bamboo, bark, banana leaves, and on pieces of earthenware. Their literature included many songs for different occasions, as well as plays, proverbs, and riddles. They also had a calendar, of twelve months for each year, seven days in a week, and thirty days for each month except December, which had 26 days. Each year had 356 days. The Filipinos also had laws to deal with serious and minor crimes, partnerships, contracts, loans, money-lending, family disputes, divorce, property rights, and inheritance. Some of these laws were written, but most were passed down by word of mouth from generation to generation. As a new law was passed, by the wise men in a village, it was announced throughout the village by a crier.

The Filipinos had a system of weights and measures, with particular units of capacity, length, and weight. Separate weights were used for light, dry goods, and heavy objects. Some of the measures used for length were the *dangkal* (the length between the tip of the thumb and the tip of the middle finger when these were stretched as far apart as possible), and the *damak* (the length of the palm).

Filipino society had three levels—the nobility, the middle-class or freemen, called *maharlika*, and the slaves, called *alipin*. People could sell themselves or their children into slavery, and all the descendants of slaves were slaves also, unless freed. Slavery was inflicted on anyone who could not pay his debts, or who committed a crime against a person in authority, or on prisoners captured in war. A slave could earn freedom by paying a large sum of money to his master, or by distinguishing himself in battle.

Filipinos were closely bound by family ties, and the father was always head of the family. Filipino women were given many privileges, and held a respected place in society. The mother named her children, and she could own and sell property. If a chieftain had no sons, his eldest daughter became chief. All women were astute traders and merchants.

The Filipinos were governed by about 30 to 100 families, each family ruling a small "kingdom" called a *barangay*. Nobles carried the title of *Gat* or *Laken*, and the highest person in the nobility was the Rajah. The people owed their

54

Rajah total obedience—they paid taxes to him, and fought his wars. The rajahs were usually able rulers, and often made agreements with other rajahs for the common welfare and protection of their people. Often several *barangays* co-operated in this way.

The Filipinos believed in a supreme god, creator of all things. Under this main god were lesser deities, sent to earth to care for the people that the supreme god had created—those of agriculture, of death, of power, of strength, of fire, of harvest, and a god who took the souls of the dead from the land of the living. Ancestors could act as agents for living people in the land of the dead. People made offerings to their ancestors, believing that these would help them in the after-life. The Filipinos strongly believed in a life after death. If a person lived his life on earth as a good citizen—perhaps as a wise, just man, or as a brave soldier—he could expect a reward in heaven. A bad citizen would be punished accordingly after death. The Filipinos believed that if a man died a natural death, which included being killed in battle, or even being eaten by a crocodile, he went to heaven. However, if he drowned, his soul stayed in the underworld, at the bottom of the sea, until many sacrifices were made to secure its release. When Filipinos of rank died, a number of slaves were killed, so that the souls of the slaves could serve the soul of their master in the other world.

The Filipinos believed that the gods could send spirits to earth—either good or evil. Forms commonly taken by these spirits were of animals, birds, reptiles, mountains, and clouds. A person who showed ill-feeling towards any of these things risked offending the gods.

The Filipinos had no special places of worship—altars were set up in caves and sacrifices made when the occasion warranted it. Each person could, and did, offer sacrifices in his own home. These took the form of sweet-smelling herbs placed in front of an idol. Each house had its own idol, of whatever spirit the householder or his family wished to placate.

At communal ceremonies of worship held by people of high rank in the community priests and priestesses, lavishly dressed in gold and silks, sacrificed pigs, which were eaten after the ceremonies. The Filipinos made offerings, often of gold or other valuables, to ensure that their requests were granted.

The ancient Filipinos did not want for much in their daily lives. They had plenty of food, and cultivated enough rice, their staple food, to tide them over any emergency. Several kinds of wine—made from palm hearts, rice, or from sugar cane—were served with meals, and on gala occasions. The rivers, streams, and sea-shores provided plenty of fish, and the forests teemed with game—deer, wild pigs, jungle-fowl, and monkeys. Daily activities were mainly concerned with gardening, hunting, fishing, trading, and fighting to defend their territory or to enlarge their Rajah's kingdom.

LANGUAGES OF THE PHILIPPINES

About 87 different languages and dialects are spoken in the Philippines. The ten main ones are Tagalog, spoken in Manila, Mindoro, and most of Luzon; Sugbuhanon, in Cebu, and parts of Mindanao; Hiligaynon, in Negros Occidental and Iloilo; Samarnon, in Samar and Leyte; Bikol, in Camarines North and South; Pampangan, in Pampanga and Tarlac; Ilocano, in La Union and Ilocos; Maquindanao, in Cotabatu; Maranao, in Lanao; and Tausug, spoken

	A		L
	I,E		M
	U,O		N
	B		NG
	D		P
	G		S
	H		T
	K		W
			Y

Two kinds of ancient Filipino writing with approximate English equivalents

55

in Jolo, parts of Zamboanga City, Basilan, other parts of Mindanao, and the Sulu Archipelago.

The languages are basically of Austronesian or Malay-Polynesian origin, but many have assimilated words from Indian, Arabic, Chinese, Spanish and English. All these influences can be seen in many words of the Tagalog language. From Sanskrit (Indian), Tagalog adopted words such as *aksaya* (waste), *katha* (compose, or write), *kuta* (fort), and others; from Arabic, *alam* (know), *salamat* (thanks), etc.; from Chinese, *ate* (elder sister), *hibi* (dried shrimps), and many food and trading words; from Spanish *mesa* (table), *silya* (chair), *kalatas* (letter), *bapor* (ship), and *pader* (wall); and from American (English), *piyer* (pier), *istraik* (strike), words for sports such as *besbol* (baseball), *boling* (bowling), *boksing* (boxing), and many more.

In 1946, Tagalog, which had been made the national language of the Philippines, became one of the three official languages, the other two being English and Spanish. In 1962, the name Tagalog was changed to Pilipino.

GROWTH OF THE ARTS

Literature: The growth of literature began centuries before the Europeans came to the Philippines, with word-of-mouth tales and legends. Writings in these early days ensured only that these legends were preserved for later years. In the days before the Spaniards, stories related the coming of many people from foreign countries to the shores of the Philippines, and simpler tales of everyday life, crops, superstitions, and religious beliefs. These stories describe people who were kindly, happy, industrious, and at home on the sea as well as on land. The talent for story-telling and writing—with tales of love, adventure, battle, visiting peoples, and everyday life—recurred for centuries. The Spanish missionaries destroyed any written works that they found, not understanding what they related, and believing them to be idolatrous.

The first book printed in the Philippines, by Spanish Catholics in 1593, was called the *Christian Doctrine*. The book was printed from wood engravings. The early literary works often had a religious theme; but non-Christian people also contributed to the literary field—people from Mindanao, the Sulu Archipelago, and the Ifugaos from the north of Luzon. Francisco Balagtas, who lived from 1789 to 1862, is recognized as the "Prince of Filipino Poets", and there are many excellent Filipino writers, some of whose works are considered classics. They usually wrote in Spanish. Perhaps the greatest of all, the national hero, Jose Rizal, wrote poems, novels and essays. His most significant work was *Mi Ultimo Adios* ("My Last Farewell"), written before he was shot by the Spaniards. Translated by Nick Joaquin, it begins:

Land that I love: Farewell: O land the sun loves:
Pearl in the sea of the Orient: Eden lost to your brood:
Gaily I go to present you this hapless, hopeless life:
Were it more brilliant: had it more freshness, more bloom:
Still for you would I give it: would give it for your good!

In barricades embattled, fighting in delirium,
Others give you their lives without doubts, without gloom.
The site nought matters: cypress, laurel or lily:
Gibbet or open field: combat or cruel martyrdom
Are equal if demanded by country and home.

I am to die when I see the heavens go vivid,
Announcing the day at last behind the dead night.
If you need colour—colour to stain that dawn with,
Let spill my blood: scatter it in good hour:
And drench in its gold one beam of the newborn light.

Woman selling pots—after a painting by Damian Domingo

During the American occupation, after the time of the Spaniards, literature began to flourish. Journalism started to become as it is today—equal to the world's best. Short stories, plays, and musical drama were created, with English now the main language of expression.

Painting and sculpture: Before European contact, the people carved figures of local animals, fish, and men and women, from wood. They wove cloth with colourful, intricate designs. The metal work of the Muslims, finely etched and carefully inlaid, goes back far into the past. When the Spaniards arrived, with Christianity, carving and decoration took a religious theme. At first the Spaniards employed Chinese sculptors for their churches—the lions outside San Agustin Church are typical of this work. The Filipinos quickly learnt, and soon took over the carving and masonry work. Spanish influence was strong, and talented Spanish sculptors came to the Philippines to teach the local people, though it was not until well into the 19th century that the Filipinos achieved any fame of their own.

57

Painters, also, were influenced by the Spaniards and other Europeans. One Filipino artist, Damian Domingo, recognized as the "Father of Filipino Painting", concentrated on miniature water-colours of Filipino people in various walks of life—potters, officials, student "dandies", fisherwomen, and market sellers. The Spaniards appointed him director of a school of fine arts, in 1826.

Shortly before the Spanish-American War, Filipino painters received recognition in Europe. When the Americans took over, they encouraged the arts, and assisted whenever they could. The School of Fine Arts of the University of the Philippines was established in 1909, and today you can find galleries along United Nations Avenue in Manila, displaying many striking paintings, both traditional and modern. A number of art colleges in Manila give excellent training, and galleries are eager to help and encourage young artists.

Not far from the centre of Manila is an artists' workshop run by Manuel Rodriguez, specializing in teaching techniques of print-making. The workshop also holds exhibitions of prints of Filipino paintings, and organizes travelling shows of these prints, and public demonstrations for students and teachers interested in graphic art.

Music: The Filipinos had many traditional forms of music before the Spaniards came, and even today the mountain people of northern Luzon play a nose-flute in the way their forefathers did centuries ago.

With the coming of the Spaniards and other Europeans, Filipino musicians learnt to appreciate the music of Western composers—Chopin, Mozart, Beethoven and others. Soon these influences began to show in Filipino music. Promising students were sent abroad, and brought back with them the atmosphere of the country where they had studied.

Such international training enabled the Filipino composers to merge the music of Western composers with the ancient melodies and rhythms of their Indo-Malayan ancestors.

EDUCATION IN THE PHILIPPINES

Everywhere the visitor goes in the Philippines, he is impressed by the number of schools and students. In the early morning hundreds of children and teen-agers, carrying text books, hurry on their way to various places of learning. In the evening, night students take their place. Manila seems to have more schools, colleges and universities than any other city I have visited.

The schools and universities: The routine of education is similar to that of Western countries. Private nurseries and kindergartens cater for the child until he reaches the age of seven, when he is eligible to enter grade one of the elementary or primary school. The pupil spends six years in the public primary schools, then attends high school for a further four years. At the end of this time the student enters a college, roughly equivalent to an Australian university. The system of education is based on that of America, providing for relatively smooth progression through the various levels. As with most developing nations, there is a passion for greater learning.

In the Philippines are some 465 separate colleges and universities, with 15 large universities in the city of Greater Manila alone. The Philippines has the second largest school and university enrolment in the world.

All studies are conducted in English from high school level onward. Before

Filipino playing a bamboo flute

58

high school the pupil, for the first two grades, uses his local dialect for all lessons, at the same time learning English and Pilipino (Tagalog), the national language, as two of his subjects. In grade three, the local dialect is dropped, and English becomes the medium of instruction, with Pilipino still a main subject. So a pupil studies at least two languages from his earliest school years.

Many courses of study are available in the Philippines. The term "college" is equivalent to the term "faculty" in Australia—thus the Philippines has a College of Liberal Arts, Arts and Sciences, Medicine, Law, Agriculture and Fisheries, and so on. The number of diplomas issued by private and public universities is regulated by the Government, but examinations to determine graduation from a college or university are not controlled to any set standard, and a wide difference exists between the actual standards reached in the two types of institutions—private and public. The Government does set a bar examination for Law students, which they must pass at the required level before they can graduate.

Private colleges, many run as private business enterprises, receive about 95% of enrolments for higher education. These schools concentrate on inexpensive courses, relying purely on lectures, without costly equipment. Sometimes there are too many graduates for the jobs available to them.

The problem of teacher-training, a difficult one in many countries, has been solved in the Philippines. For a number of years, teachers here have been chosen from applicants with four years of college education and a Bachelor of Arts degree. Teachers usually continue studying for higher qualification in their spare time.

Educational television and radio: Educational television is widely used in the cities of the northern Philippines. The Ateneo University at Loyola Heights in Quezon City, using closed-circuit television for its own area, also sends programmes by micro-wave to one of the television stations in Manila, from where they are forwarded by general transmission to elementary and high schools.

The Bureau of Public Schools also operates a radio educational system— the biggest in South East Asia. The transistor radio plays a very big part in this scheme, because many public school children carry transistors. Children can thus receive instruction by radio wherever they are, especially in outlying communities. The Government has been considering distribution of radio sets to outlying villages (similar to the system adopted in Papua and New Guinea). The Philippines makes its own transistors, and these will be used when this system is put into operation.

In the early morning, before the farmer goes to work, radio stations broadcast public information and adult education programmes, on agriculture, especially food production, and these are proving successful.

GAMES AND SPORTS

The Filipinos enjoy sports—either as spectators or players. As well as many popular Western sports, such as golf, bowls, horse-racing, baseball, and boxing, the Filipinos have adopted more unusual games, some peculiar to the Philippines.

Jai-alai

59

Jai-alai: Jai-alai (pronounced "high-lie") one of the most fascinating games I have ever seen, and also one of the fastest, is played at a stadium. Onlookers watch from the comfort of the Skyroom, or go below to mix with the dense crowd, amid an excited chatter of conversation, the shouting of bettors, and bookmakers, and a pall of cigarette smoke.

Jai-alai originated in the Basque country of Spain, and was brought by the Spaniards to the Philippines. It stemmed from handball, and still bears some similarity to handball and squash, but is much faster than either. Once the players, called *pelotari*, all came from Spain, and commanded very high wages. Today the Filipinos play just as well as the Spaniards.

The players have a basket, shaped like a long scoop, attached to their hand. This scoop, in which the ball is caught, has a glove fitted to one end, called a *cesta*. The player catches the ball in the basket and hurls it back in such a way that the other player has difficulty in catching it. The ball, called the *pelota*, travels at about 150 miles an hour, and bounces very high, the player leaping up after it.

Sipa: Similar in some ways to badminton and tennis, sipa is played either as a singles or a doubles match. The ball, made of rattan and hollow inside, is about four inches in diameter. It is kept going continuously, and cannot be touched with any part of the body except knees, legs, and feet. It bounces like a tennis ball, and is kicked backwards and forwards over a net until a point is scored. The court is also like that used for tennis.

Arnis de mano: An exciting sport—actually a style of fencing found only in the Philippines. Two contestants are armed with two sticks each, and a player has to prevent his opponent from hitting him. Fair and foul blows are recognized, and only fair blows—those above the waist—are scored. Each bout lasts three or four rounds, each of three minutes. No protective covering is worn.

Cockfighting: Like England's fox-hunts, and Spain's bull-fights, cockfighting is a blood-sport constantly under attack by animal-loving people. Nevertheless, it has a huge following in the Philippines, where every city has a cock-pit —the larger cities more than one. Cockfighting is legal, but the sport must be held in a place away from the general business area. Crowds of people watch the fights, in an enclosed cock-pit or an open makeshift one. The pits look

COLOUR

A temple in the Chinese Cemetery on the outskirts of Manila

One of the reception rooms at Malacañang Palace, the home of the President

Market sellers are part of the Philippine way of life

Jeepneys are custom-built to any requirement

like miniature stadiums. Tiered seats rise from floor level almost to the roof, looking down on a wired-off arena. Cockfights are sometimes hard for the visitor to find, unless he knows how they are advertised. The recognized sign that fights are on is a red flag hanging across the street—no other advertising is used.

Before a fight, the spectator is bombarded with sound—the crowing of cocks, the excited chatter of many people, and the loud, rapid calling of bets. Meals can be bought at the pit, and many people stay from the opening of the fights, at eight in the morning, to midnight, when the pit closes. In the breaks of about five minutes between fights fortunes are won and lost. Betting ranges from 100 pesos (about U.S.$25), to 100,000 pesos (about U.S.$25,000). Bookmakers write nothing down, but keep mental calculations of how much they have laid out, the odds quoted, and to whom. The bookmaker has a fantastic memory, and usually works for a syndicate, which provides his money. He attends thousands of cockfights, and knows every aspect of the sport. Odds are determined by the progress of the fight. Each game starts with even money, and fluctuates during the fight depending on what bird the bettor has backed. Towards the end, the odds on an apparently-losing bird can go up as high as four to one. About 1,000 people attend each fight. Admission costs 50 cent-avos (about U.S.10 cents), or twice this if you want to watch from the gallery.

Many Filipino families raise fighting cocks, and it is common to see one of these birds tied by a leg-rope outside a house. Rearing a good fighting cock is no easy task, and the bird's owner lavishes constant care and attention, often treating the bird almost as one of his children. It takes four to five months of daily training to bring a good bird up to the standard required for a public cockfight. Training begins in the morning, with a bath of vinegar and wine. The bird is then exercised, and at least once each day is made to fight other birds.

When the bird is in peak condition, he is taken with pride to the arena. Before the contest, the two adversaries are shown to the spectators, and initial bets are laid. To stir each bird up, the head of one cock is held in the hand, with the neck outstretched for the other bird to peck. After a few minutes, the other bird has its neck pecked. Then a long steel spur, blade-like and razor-sharp, is attached to the left leg of each bird. I was told that this spur is dipped in a poison to speed up the contest.

The birds fight viciously, until one is killed. If they both sink to the ground, exhausted, they are held up to one another and then dropped, to see if they can still fight. This may be done several times before the fight is declared over. If both birds die, the one that dies first loses. The losing bird is given to the owner of the winning one, and then cooked and eaten. Any poison—only skin-deep—is cut out before cooking.

Cockfighting has been a favourite sport in the Philippines for hundreds of years—long before the arrival of Europeans.

GROWTH OF

THE REPUBLIC

The Philippines had been a major port of call for Arab traders plying between the Moluccas and China since the 9th century. During the reign of the Sung and Ming dynasties in China, many Chinese began to trade with the Philippines, and Chinese colonies appeared on the coasts and slightly inland. By the middle of the 14th century, other Eastern countries threatened China's trade. Between 1405 and 1417, the Ming emperor Yung Lo sent a fleet of about 60 ships to visit Lingayen, Manila Bay, Mindoro and Sulu, to try and regain control of Philippines trade. China established a brief rule over Luzon, until the death of Yung Lo.

In the 15th century, Muslims spread to the Philippines from the Moluccas, gaining control over most of the southern islands, and forcing the Chinese to trade only with the northern islands. Later the Muslims allowed the Chinese to resume trade in areas under Muslim influence. When the Spaniards arrived, Muslim Filipinos were actively trading with the Chinese and Indo-Chinese.

THE SPANIARDS

Although Ferdinand Magellan discovered the Philippines in 1521, it was not until 1565 that the Spaniards, under Miguel Lopez de Legazpi, founded a colony on Cebu, calling the whole group of islands Filipinas, after King Philip II of Spain. The Spanish explorer Andres de Urdaneta had by this time discovered a passage westwards across the Pacific from Acapulco, making colonization of the Philippines a profitable venture. The passage Urdaneta found was used by a ship *Acapulco Galleon*, which provided a yearly service to the Philippines from Mexico until the end of the 18th century.

Early settlement in the Philippines was primarily a military and missionary venture, and could have been hindered partly by the exploits of Sir Francis Drake, the English seaman who played havoc with Spanish ships in the Mexican and Peruvian regions and returned with Spanish treasure to Britain.

Colonization of the islands: The Spaniards first arrived in the Philippines from Mexico, via Cape Horn. The Spanish administrators at Manila, chosen as the capital by Legazpi, prospered through heavy taxes levied on the outlying districts.

The Spaniards established a feudal land system, under which the Filipinos, or *Indios* as the Spaniards called them, did all the hard labour. The arrogance of the newcomers turned the natural hospitality of the Filipinos to hatred.

The Spaniards were not concerned, at this stage, by the rebelliousness of some groups of Filipinos, because as yet the people of the islands lived in small tribal and regional groups, with no sense of national unity.

However, many foreign powers threatened the Spanish colony during the early years of settlement—mainly the Portuguese, Dutch, Chinese, and Japanese. The Spaniards successfully resisted Portuguese efforts to drive them from Cebu. Later the Spanish King annexed Portugal to Spain, closing Portuguese ports to the Dutch traders, who then sought new trading centres in the East Indies. Soon the Dutch were plundering Spanish vessels in the Philippines. In the first half of the 17th century, repeated Dutch attacks were made on Manila, but all were successfully dealt with by the Spaniards, with Filipino warriors.

Meanwhile, the Chinese in Manila posed an internal threat to Spanish administration. The Spanish were worried by the economic success of the

66

Chinese. The Government who had already compelled all Chinese to live in a separate compound, called the *Parian,* now began to levy heavy taxes on them, and treated them very harshly. The seemingly endless patience of the Chinese finally broke in 1603, and they rose in revolt, burning buildings and attacking inhabitants of the Quiapo and Tondo districts of Manila. The Spanish, again with loyal Filipino troops, quelled the uprising. By 1639 the Chinese population had grown to 28,000. Revolts took place in 1639, 1662, and 1762, but all were repressed.

The Japanese, who formed quite large, but scattered colonies in Manila, and in the provinces of Bulacan, La Union, and Cagayan, also revolted, aiding the small bands of Filipino rebels, but all uprisings were put down by combined Spanish and pro-Spanish Filipino forces.

In the Seven Years' War, from 1756 to 1763, when England, Russia and Hanover (Germany) were at war with France, Austria, and Spain, the British captured Manila; but by the Treaty of Paris, in 1763, Spain regained the Philippines and Cuba, in exchange for Florida and concessions in the Honduras.

The Spaniards stifled Filipino culture, using the Filipinos at first only for hard labour. Their aim was to colonize, and to enforce Spanish law and administration—to make the Filipinos into Spaniards. Mixed families of Spanish and Filipino blood were not looked down upon, for the Spaniards thought people with a little Spanish blood were better than those with none at all. Many mixed-race people, called *mestizos,* were given responsible Government positions, and accepted at the highest levels of Spanish society.

Catholic friars, some recruited from Mexico and Peru, tried to convert the people to Christianity. Hundreds of these friars—Dominican, Augustinian and Franciscan—entered the Philippines to instruct the Filipinos in education and religion.

The people were organized into village units called *barrios,* with a system of local government controlled by a Spanish administrator. Both the Spanish Government and the Church were ignored by the mountain people of northern Luzon and the Muslims of the south. The reaction of the Muslims was as fierce as that displayed by the Moors to the Spaniards, and the Spaniards called the Muslims *Moros*—a name they do not like.

Large estates were given to Spanish and part-Spanish families. The former owners of this land—the Filipinos—became tenants, who served the new landlords and farmed their ground. In this way a large number of Spanish and part-Spanish people became very wealthy.

The Philippines was a testing ground for conversion of Asian countries to Christianity. In fact, Santo Tomas University was opened for the primary purpose of training young priests for missionary work in China and Japan. It was not at first intended as an institute of learning for the Filipinos.

Beginnings of national unity: Spanish rule in the Philippines lasted 333 years, and by the 19th century the Filipinos were beginning to feel a sense of national unity. By now many Filipinos had mixtures of Spanish or Chinese blood— the Chinese had found that by marrying Filipinos they were assured permanent residence in the Philippines—and the levels in society had become so ill-defined that in 1849 all Filipinos had been ordered to adopt Spanish names. In 1882, the Philippines had over six million people, the majority Catholics.

The patient water buffalo—for centuries the friend of the farmer

67

With over 2,000 schools, colleges, and other places of learning such as navy and military schools and art academies, most of these people could at least read and write. Filipinos occupied high positions in local government, with staff under them to perform most of their administrative duties (though the Spanish Governor-General was still in supreme command). This system seemed to work quite well on the surface, but the Filipinos were well aware that Spain was more concerned in easing her administrative load than making conditions better for the Filipinos.

An incident that sparked off intense distrust and ultimately the overthrow of the Spanish Government had occurred in 1872, when a number of people, supported by three Filipino priests, complained to the Spanish authorities that they were not paid adequately for their work, and that they were paying unjust taxes. The protest was received as a revolt against the Spanish system, the priests arrested and executed, along with other Filipinos guilty of the so-called "revolt". This action stirred up the first really large-scale resentment against the Spaniards, which simmered for a number of years.

In 1882, a Filipino movement known as the *Propaganda* was established, to campaign for reforms, equality of speech, and freedom of the press. The organization did not urge independence, but wanted the Philippines made a province of Spain. At the same time, many Filipinos were studying in France and Spain, and the French Revolution had given these people hope for the liberation of their country from the Spaniards. The ideas of these students had reached the Philippines themselves, and were becoming widespread. By 1884, reports were received by the Philippine administration that a group of people with money and arms were preparing to overthrow the Spaniards in the Philippines. These reports came not only from France and Spain, but from America and England—in fact from all places overseas where Filipinos were studying. The reasons for discontent were given as "corrupt officials", "disproportionate taxes" and other abuses. The Spaniards, by now quite alarmed, tried to stamp out any such causes of dissatisfaction. Some reforms took place, including a scheme for free medicine introduced in 1884. The tribute to Spain was abolished, and replaced by a head tax, paid by all Filipinos 18 years old and over.

About this time, three important men became active in the development of the Philippines. . . .

Jose Rizal

Doctor Jose Rizal: Rizal was born in 1861, and at the age of only three years, wrote his first poem. He graduated in 1877 as a Bachelor of Arts, and entered Medical School at Santo Tomas University. He was a brilliant student, and at 18 already winning acclaim for his writings. He went to Spain in 1882, where he studied painting, sculpture, English, German, and Arabic. While overseas he discussed earnestly with other Filipino students in Europe the future of his homeland; but Rizal hoped for greater unity between Spain and the Philippines. At 26, he could speak Spanish, Latin, French, English, German, Italian, Dutch, Arabic, Greek, Sanskrit, and Hebrew—as well as his native Tagalog. He lectured at a German university in the German language. He also had some knowledge of Swedish and Portuguese. He graduated as a licentiate of the University of Madrid, and was called Doctor, though he actually practised ophthalmology, not having submitted a thesis in medicine. He was a writer of renown, and could perhaps be classified as a genius.

68

Andres Bonifacio: Bonifacio was born in 1863, eldest of six children. His education terminated in primary school. He made and sold canes, and painted posters for business firms. An avid reader, he taught himself Spanish, and founded a dramatic club. With his ability for leadership and great courage, it was not long before he took part in shaping the destiny of his nation.

Hadji Butu: Butu was born in 1865, and had mastered the Koran by the time he was six. At the age of twelve, when he was fluent in Arabic, he drafted and signed, on behalf of his Muslim people, a peace treaty with the Spaniards, and at 15, he was the leader of the Muslim sultans. Though he fought both Spaniards and Americans, and claimed that no power could subjugate the Muslims, he was the guiding force in making the Muslim people part of the Philippine nation. He later negotiated friendship between the Americans and Muslims, and in 1904 joined the Government. He became a senator on many occasions, between 1916 and 1931, and died, of natural causes, in 1939, aged 74.

The Spanish-Filipino War: In 1885, Spain was given sovereignty of the Jolo Archipelago at the southern end of the Philippines, in return for Borneo (which at one time belonged to the Sultan of Jolo, and lies only a few miles from the Jolo Archipelago). Also in 1885, Germany left the Carolines, giving control of these islands to Spain. Next year, wars broke out again between the Spaniards and the Muslims of Mindanao. The Spanish Governor, realizing that his men were getting nowhere with the Muslims, and that trying to subdue these people with arms was an impossible task, finally recommended that the Muslims be left alone, to follow their own religion, giving as his main reason "fighting is not a Christian action".

Doctor Rizal, in Spain at this time to further his studies, joined fellow Filipino students in a movement to achieve improved conditions for his people, and tried to awaken the Spaniards to the situation in the Philippines. He wrote a novel called *Noli Me Tangere* (translated *Touch Me Not*), showing the life of the Spaniards and Filipinos in the Philippines. He intended to point out in this book the problems existing in his country, and their possible solutions. He said in the book that he would not be a party to any conspiracy, but the Manila Government put him under close watch when he returned to the Philippines in 1887, and the book was banned in the Philippines because the Government thought it had a revolutionary theme.

Rizal went overseas again—to America and Europe. Five years later, in Hong Kong, he was asked to correct some writings that told of the activities of the friars in the Philippines. Rizal's writing career was shortly to end. Returning to Manila, he attended a meeting to establish a society called the *Liga Filipina*, which aimed to unite the Philippines into a national body and to define any injustices or violence. Not long after the society was formed, Rizal was arrested and sent in exile to Dapitan, on the northern coast of Mindanao.

In 1896, the society of *Kataastaasan Kagalanggalangang Katipunan* (translated as *Society of the Sons of the People*), formed secretly in 1892 with Andres Bonifacio as president, held a meeting and decided to buy arms and ammunition from Japan. Unlike the *Liga Filipina*, the *Katipunan* society believed that revolution was the only way to achieve Philippine independence. They were eager to make contact with Jose Rizal in Dapitan, and enlist his aid. The man selected to do this was Dr Valenzuela, who under the name of "Mr Bonifacio", with a blind companion, set out for Dapitan. The society were careful not to alert the Spaniards, who thought "Mr Bonifacio" was merely bringing the blind man to Dapitan for treatment.

Rizal would have nothing to do with the *Katipunan*, and still firmly believed that the Philippines and Spain should be closer united. When the emissary suggested that at least the *Katipunan* should send a party of raiders to free him from exile, Rizal again disagreed. His visitor left the next day. The *Katipunan*, told of Rizal's refusal, decided to still go ahead with their plans for revolt, and also to free Rizal from Dapitan, against his wishes.

Rizal wrote to the Spanish Governor offering to help Spain in the uprising in Cuba. His offer was accepted, but before he could sail the *Katipunan* staged their attempted rescue. Rizal refused their aid again, and sailed for Spain, en route to Cuba. Before reaching Spain, however, Rizal was arrested and brought back to Manila, where he was imprisoned in Fort Santiago, in the walled city of Intramuros. The Spaniards knew of the activities of the *Katipunan*, and filled the gaols with suspected members. Martial law was declared. On 25th August, 1896, Bonifacio at a secret meeting of the society was told that Spanish soldiers were approaching to attack. Shots rang out, and Bonifacio led his men against the Spanish troops, in the first skirmish of the revolution.

Bonifacio, very thorough in planning his campaign, fought many successful minor battles against the Spaniards. The Government soon realized how powerful the resistance was, and declared a state of war in eight provinces. The revolt spread like wildfire to other provinces, and for the first time the Filipinos united as a formidable force, under General Emilio Aguinaldo. Spain sent 2,000 troops to help quell the uprising, but to no avail. Aguinaldo showed himself to be an excellent military leader, and the reinforcements from Spain in no way slowed the impetus of the revolutionary campaign. The rebels fought with Mauser rifles—and when these were unavailable, with sticks, poles, spears, and bows and arrows.

In November 1896 Rizal's trial began. Denying to the end having given any support to the revolution, Rizal reaffirmed that his only aim was greater solidarity and unity between the Filipinos and the Spaniards. His protests were in vain, and the Spaniards sentenced him to death. On the 30th December he was marched from Fort Santiago at 6.30 in the morning for execution. Told he was to be shot in the back, Rizal protested, asking that the firing squad should be in front of him.

Rizal's death, at only 35 years of age, had far-reaching effects. It spurred the rebels on, and was received with dismay by Filipino students abroad. Shortly after the execution, Filipinos in Hong Kong drafted reports of injustices to Filipinos by the Spaniards, and requested intervention by England, Germany, America or France. The respective officials of these countries in Hong Kong refused to send these reports, and the British official told the Filipinos not to jeopardize British hospitality in Hong Kong. The Filipinos, undeterred, mailed the requests direct, but to no avail. The great powers ignored the Filipinos' sufferings.

Meanwhile battles in the Philippines continued. Bonifacio had by this time drifted apart from Aguinaldo, and planned to set up his own government, with its own army; the rebels had elected Aguinaldo their president. Bonifacio, now 34 years old, was captured by the Spaniards, court-martialled for treason, and sentenced to death. At the place of execution, he tried to run, and was shot down.

In December, 1897, a pact of truce was signed by the Filipinos and Spaniards, resulting in General Aguinaldo's voluntary exile to Hong Kong. Peace reigned on the surface, but underneath dwelt a feeling of continued uneasiness and distrust. The Spanish, under cover of the truce, tried to consolidate their position in the Philippines, while in Hong Kong General Aguinaldo bought arms and enlisted American aid for a renewed effort to overthrow the Spaniards.

THE AMERICANS

In 1898 the Spanish Government received information that in the event of a war between Spain and America, the Philippines would be the first place the Americans would attack. Local peace was broken in April, when an uprising occurred in the south. America sailed to attack the Philippines. Aguinaldo, meanwhile, had extracted a promise from an American commodore, George Dewey, that America would recognize Philippines independence, and that Aguinaldo would lead the Filipinos and create his own government. The Americans promised that the Philippines would be a centralized republic, under the protection of America.

Spanish withdrawal from the Philippines: At 5.00 a.m. on 1st May, 1898, the American Fleet, under Commodore Dewey, arrived in Manila Bay, and defeated the Spanish defenders. Numerous battles were fought between the Spanish and the American-Filipino forces. Before long, the Filipinos drove the Spaniards from many provinces and besieged Manila.

Spain, by now only too ready to be rid of the troublesome Filipinos, secretly agreed to surrender to the Americans, insisting only that Spanish property be protected. The Spaniards and Americans agreed to stage a mock-battle for Manila. With the exchange of a few token shots, on 13th August, 1898, the Spanish surrendered the city of Manila.

In November of that year, President McKinley informed Spain that if the American proposal to annex the Philippines was not accepted, America would attack Spain herself. The Spaniards wanted the case put to arbitration, but when America then offered Spain 20 million dollars in exchange for the Philippines, Spain accepted.

Before the treaty was signed between Spain and America, President McKinley described the United States' task in the Philippines as one of "benevolent assimilation"; but his orders to the American Army were to gain American sovereignty over the Philippines at all costs—by force if necessary. Aguinaldo was sworn in as President, as agreed to earlier, but feelings towards the Americans were not cordial. The Filipinos had won a battle for freedom, and were not going to be put under the yoke of a foreign power again. As a Catholic nation (or ardent Muslim, in the south), they refused to be converted to any other faith; this annoyed the American Protestant missionaries pouring hopefully into the Philippines.

The Filipino-American War: With such an undercurrent of resentment, it was no time at all before misunderstandings arose, leading finally to a Filipino

71

being shot by an American on San Juan Bridge. This sparked off another war, between the Filipinos, again led by General Aguinaldo, and the Americans. Before it ended, Americans behaved often in the exact way the Spaniards had, during their regime, and provoked just as much animosity. Finally, in 1901, Aguinaldo was tricked and caught. The General had sent for reinforcements and, when a party of soldiers arrived, thought that these were the aid he had requested. Unknown to him, his position had been betrayed to the Americans. The so-called "reinforcements" captured Aguinaldo and took him to Manila.

On 19th April, 1901, Aguinaldo took the Oath of Allegiance to the United States, and the war was officially over, though this was not fully effective until September of that year. The war had lasted a little over three years, and had cost America some 600 million dollars, and the use of very many men. People asked at the time why American intervention ever took place. Some reasons given were that the Philippines presented a good market for American products, a good site for a naval base, and a stepping-stone to American trade with Asia. Others suggested that America wanted to emulate Britain and build up an empire of her own.

American administration: Within a few days of the official American take-over, English became the main language in the schools. The Americans revised administration, established education on a far greater scale, and severed connection between the church and the government. An electoral system based on the American was established and a public service began operation.

Limits were placed on exports of manufactured goods from the Philippines, but not on American imports. The Americans did nothing about expanding manufacture of Philippine products, but mining, for American gain, was developed. The import-export system caused products to be grown for export to the detriment of home-grown food crops. The Philippines soon became a nation of agriculturalists not able to save enough food for their own use.

The Americans nevertheless discontinued the head tax and forced labour. They began land reforms, and taxed land according to acreages. In 1907, the first elections were held, putting the Nationalista Party into power. Ten years later a Legislative Assembly was formed, composed of a House of Representatives and a Senate. The nation was on its way to becoming independent. In 1935 the Government of the Commonwealth of the Philippines was formed and America withdrew its Governor-General. Manuel Quezon was the first President under this new system. The American Governor-General, now appointed United States High Commissioner, moved from Malacañang Palace to allow Quezon to take residence. The future of the Philippines now seemed assured, but another force seemed ready to strike. Japan was on the march.

Japanese occupation: In 1941 America learned that Japan was likely to attack Pearl Harbour. This was treated as a joke by many people in the United States, but military preparations were made in the Philippines in case there was any truth in the report. Japan struck Pearl Harbour on 7th December, 1942, and the next day attacked the Philippines.

Manila was subjected to daily bombings and Japanese troops landed on

Manuel Quezon

The Las Piñas bamboo organ

*Handcarved woodwork in the choir loft
of San Agustin Church, in Manila*

*The lectern and original missal at San
Agustin Church*

The University of the Philippines at Quezon City

Entrance to Santo Tomas University, founded in 1611 in Manila

Filipino artists have received world
acclaim for their work

Father, daughter, and suitor, a monument to old Filipino custom

79

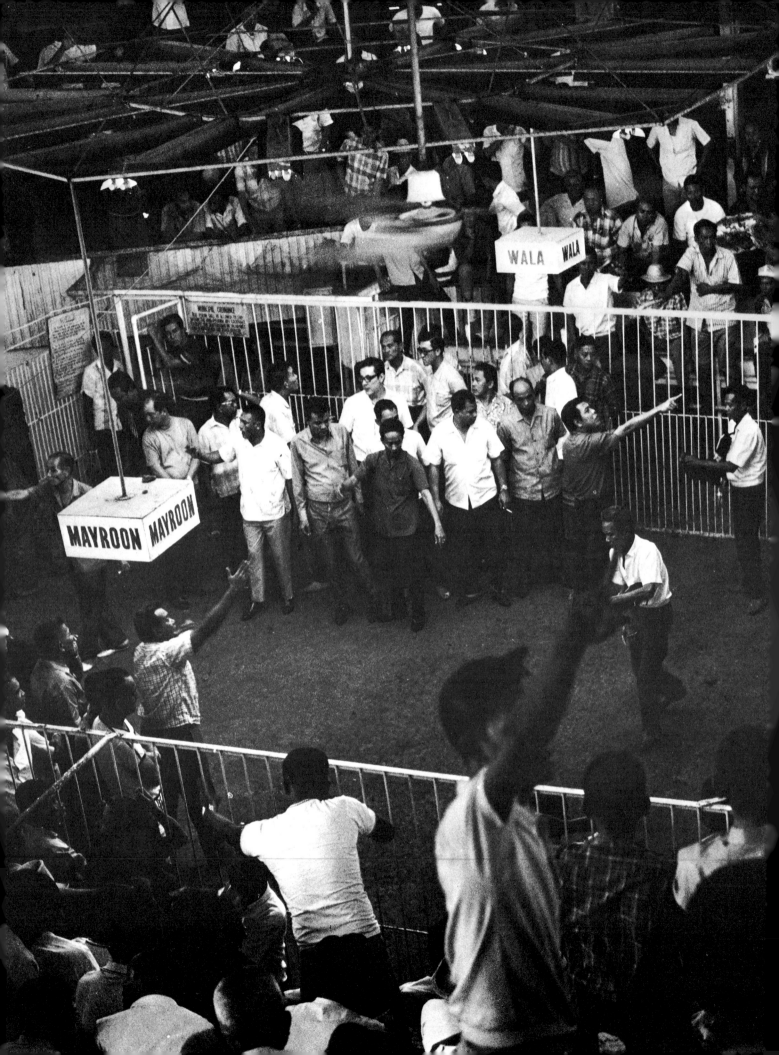

Arnis de mano, a Philippine style of fencing, using two sticks

The cockfight is part of the Filipino way of life

Filipino architecture is noted for its murals

Playing sipa, or Filipino foot tennis, with a rattan ball

Fort Santiago, in the walled city of
Intramuros

Part of the old Spanish walled city of
Intramuros, in Manila

85

*The American war memorial about six
miles from Manila*

*The administrative block at Mala-
cañang Palace, home of the President*

The terrace at Malacañang Palace,
overlooking the estate

Luzon, north and south of Manila, within a few days of the initial attack. The American Army moved to Bataan and Corregidor, and President Quezon went also. Manila, declared an open city, was occupied by the Japanese on 2nd January, 1942. (They remained in Manila until February, 1945.) The battle for Bataan and Corregidor took place, and General MacArthur, with President Quezon, left for Australia. General Wainwright made a heroic stand against the Japanese, holding out for five months, but was finally defeated.

The Japanese, after interning all American citizens in Santo Tomas University, registered all vehicles and took stock of all available fuel supplies. All radio sets had to be surrendered, for adjustment to prevent short wave broadcasts. Japanese currency was introduced. All houses and dwellings were searched. Schools remained open, but under stringent control. Food was short, and medical supplies almost non-existent. An active Filipino resistance movement spread throughout the islands. From a small start, the Resistance eventually became a large scale operation, attacking the Japanese and making sabotage raids. The guerrillas, Americans, Australians, and Filipinos, included a group called the Anti-Japanese People's Army, or *Hukbalahap*, shortened to *Huks* (pronounced "Hooks").

The wartime president, Quezon, continued to run his government in exile, from the United States, but in the Philippines government was strictly under Japanese control. The Prime Minister of Japan came to Manila to tell the Filipinos that the Japanese meant them to have independence, but the people took this news with no show of enthusiasm; they did not want independence as dictated by the invaders.

By this time units of the Japanese Army began to retreat for the first time —pursued, by the Australians in New Guinea, along the Kokoda Trail. This gave the *Huks* their first real hope for liberation of the Philippines. By 1944 the tide of battle had turned; Americans, Australians and allied forces were on their way north. From their headquarters at Manila, the Japanese had nearly a million men scattered throughout the war zones.

In August, 1944, President Quezon died, and was replaced by President Osmeña.

In September, Mindanao was bombed by the Allies. Later 1,000 allied bombers hit Manila. Landings on Leyte were made in October. The Japanese Navy attacked the American and Australian warships supporting the landings, but were defeated. The process of liberation slowly began. In the Battle of Manila, the city and its people suffered terribly. The walled city of Intramuros was almost destroyed, and many other beautiful buildings were destroyed or damaged, but on 27th February, 1945, a victorious General MacArthur handed over the Philippines to President Osmeña, and the return to normal living began.

AFTER WORLD WAR II

Economic aid from America was badly needed to bring about the recovery of the Philippines from the damage and destruction of World War II. A somewhat difficult situation, resulting from bad management of aid, and misuse of currency and import restrictions, began in 1950: imports of luxury goods, and food that could have been produced in the Philippines itself, led to a further request for American aid. The Philippines Government

F

received a proposal for a five-year plan costing 250 million dollars, to improve the nation's economy. Americans were to provide technical assistance in agriculture and other fields.

The Americans were not happy with the feudal-type land systems in the Philippines, and advised agrarian reform. The Philippine Government became annoyed at this, particularly since the United States had made no efforts to alter the same agricultural situation during the 48 years of their administration.

The Philippines granted military bases to the United States in return for a promise of United States protection in the event of another attack on the Philippines.

Government after the war: The Philippines became an independent republic on 4th July, 1946. The Nationalista Party realized that Osmeña was not powerful enough to hold the party together, and he lost office in the 1946 elections to General Roxas—who had played a prominent part within (though opposed to) the government set up by the Japanese. A diplomatic leader, Roxas was favoured by the Americans, but he died in 1948. Quirino, the Vice-President, took over, but unlike Roxas, this leader did nothing about reform—vital in the Philippines at that time.

At the next elections Laurel, the man earlier appointed President by the Japanese, stood for office. The elections, marked by corruption and violence, put Quirino back into power. His victory was violently disputed, many people claiming that proper counts of votes should have given the presidency to Laurel, and the four years of Quirino's term were marked by unrest and constant suspicion of corrupt government. A former wartime Resistance, the *Huks*, now controlled by Communist guerrillas, threatened to start another revolution, and bandits made it unsafe to travel on roads in remote areas. The Secretary of Defence, Ramon Magsaysay, who had led Filipinos against the Japanese Occupation, argued that reforms, on a large scale, were the only way to satisfy the Filipinos and stifle Communist progress. He tried himself to instigate the reforms necessary, and some of these were successful, but the constant shortcomings, weaknesses, and opposition of the Quirino Government forced Magsaysay to resign. Later he stood as presidential candidate himself, and was elected.

To prove his faith in the Filipino people, Magsaysay opened the Malacañang Palace to the public, allowing anyone to visit it, and walk around the grounds. The palace is still open to visitors. Magsaysay made sweeping reforms, gradually lessening the hostility of the *Huks*, and took decisive action in the formation of S.E.A.T.O. (the South East Asia Treaty Organization, between Australia, New Zealand, Pakistan, the Philippines, Thailand, and the United States), which Quirino had been toying with for some time.

In March 1957, Magsaysay was killed in an air crash, plunging the Philippine nation into confusion and grief. Vice-President Garcia took his place, followed by Macapagal, in 1961, and then President Ferdinand Marcos in 1966.

Ramon Magsaysay

Structure of the Government today: Since the establishment of the Republic of the Philippines, in 1935, the Government has been acting under a Constitution similar to that of the United States.

90

The President has executive powers. His appointment depends on the result of elections, by qualified voters. He holds office for a period of four years, and can stand for re-election at the end of this term if he wishes. His official residence is Malacañang Palace. The President is the head of all departments and offices of the Government including defence services. He has general supervision over local government, and ensures that all laws are carried out. A great deal of the task of government nevertheless falls to the Executive Secretary, whose position is permanent, and not controlled by elections.

The Philippine National Flag: The history of the Philippine National Flag goes back to 1892, when Andres Bonifacio designed a flag (in those days a war banner) for his revolutionary group. This was a rectangular piece of red cloth, with three Ks, symbolic of Kataastaasan Kagalanggalangang Katipunan, arranged in a triangle in the centre. All the members of Bonifacio's society signed their names to its original constitution in their blood, which may explain the choice of red for the basic colour of the flag. Bonifacio experimented with the banner, and before the 1896 revolution asked the women of his Society to design another red flag, with the three white Ks in a line at the bottom of the flag, and a rayed white sun in the middle of the top portion.

At the same time, General Aguinaldo designed a flag with a stylized, eight-rayed white sun, denoting the eight provinces that first resisted the Spaniards. Inside the sun, a K was drawn, in Tagalog script. After the truce, while in Hong Kong, Aguinaldo designed a new flag, and asked some Filipino women in the British colony to make it up. These women—Marcela Agoncillo, her eldest daughter Lorenza, and Delfina Herboza, Rizal's niece, sewed the flag which became the National Flag of the Philippines.

The flag consists of two rectangular pieces—royal blue, for universality, and red, to symbolize the Filipino's willingness to shed his blood for his country. At the left side is a white triangular insert, containing in its centre a golden sun with eight rays, symbolizing the eight heroic provinces, and at each corner of the equilateral triangle, a gold, five-pointed star, representing one of the three main divisions of the Philippines—the Visayas, Luzon, and Mindanao. The edge of the flag is bound in gold. The flag was first displayed in the Philippines on 28th May, 1898, to commemorate the Philippine victory against the Spaniards in the Battle of Alapan. Aguinaldo stipulated that in times of war, the flag was to be placed with the red section at the top, and in times of peace, the blue was to be uppermost.

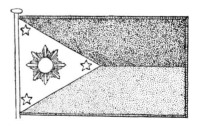

National Flag of the Philippines

91

A WEALTH OF GOODS

The Philippine population of 33 million is growing at an annual rate of more than 3%, which means that there are about a million more mouths to feed each year, and this rate is increasing. However it has been estimated that the country, with full agricultural production, can sustain about 80 million people. More than a half of the total land area is suitable for agriculture, or timber production, and land suitable for farming is some 20 million acres.

AGRICULTURE

The main crop in the Philippines is rice, but other important products are sugar, abaca, tobacco, pineapples, cotton, copra, meat, and dairy goods. Cattle, mainly of Indian and Asian origin, pigs, and poultry, are raised.

The farmer today: Farms are usually small—about eight or nine acres, but some are as large as 45 acres. Some farmers do not own the land they work, but lease it from the owners. About 40% of farms are leasehold. Of the total population, some three quarters rely basically on farming for their livelihood, and about 61% of the Philippine work force are engaged in some agricultural pursuit—farming, fishing, logging, or hunting.

The usual measure of land in the Philippines is the hectare, approximately equal to two and a half acres; and the usual measure for rice grain and other crops is the cavan, equal to two and a half bushels. Mechanization plays a big part in agriculture, and to offset any problems of unemployment through this, the Government has established homestead farms in some places. The unemployed farmer is given a block of land—of up to 60 acres—which he can farm himself.

With farming on a fairly small scale, the farmer has to augment his income during slack periods, usually by raising a few pigs, water buffalo, or cattle; by handicrafts; by selling firewood, raising poultry, or fishing. The average rice farmer works about 125 days a year on the rice crop itself, and takes about 300 hours to farm a hectare without machinery, so he usually has from six to nine months each year to devote to other agricultural pursuits.

More than a quarter of the rice-growing area in the Philippines is served by irrigation—whether for high, low or swampy ground. The most effective system is the gravity feed system from dams, for all-the-year irrigation, but other systems operate—such as pumping from deep wells. Irrigated crops produce a higher yield.

The Government regulates by law the supply and distribution of fertilizer in agricultural regions. Fertilizer, subsidized by the Government, is sold to the farmer through co-operatives, at a price he can easily afford. Local fertilizer is used as far as possible, but this is not sufficient to meet demand, and additional supplies must be imported from time to time.

92

Research: Research in agriculture is extensive, covering a wide area of rural activities, from soil conservation to stock breeding and better-yielding, more resistant crops, particularly rice. All aspects of scientific farming are covered by various Government-financed experimental stations; and the Ford and Rockefeller foundations also finance a big research centre, with the co-operation of the Philippine Government. The centre, called the International Rice Research Institute, is concerned with evolving a new, more productive, nutritious variety of rice plant for the benefit of all rice-producing countries, and trains students from all over the world.

Forestry: At least half a million people in the Philippines depend on the timber industry for their livelihood; and the country is one of the largest lumber producers in the world. Of about 1,000 kinds of commercial timber growing in Philippine forests, less than 200 are marketed, so the industry has plenty of room for expansion. Timber from trees such as narra, tindalo, camagon, molave, ipil, yakal, banuyo, akle, guijo, tiaong or "Philippine mahogany", lauan, tangile, almon, bagtikan and mayapis is exported. Philippine forests also yield pine (from the high areas of Luzon), rattan, cutch, resins, oils, beeswax, guttapercha, medicinal plants (such as those giving quinine, used in the treatment of malaria), charcoal, and firewood. Narra, the Philippines National Tree, ranks as one of the best cabinet-making timbers in the world. About five other timbers are grown for pulp and paper manufacture.

Forestry research has brought excellent results. Melina, a native of Northern Rhodesia, was introduced to the Philippines in 1960. One of the fastest-growing hardwoods known, this tree is self-pruning, and grows at a rate of 16 to 25 feet every three years, reaching a final height of about 66 feet. It is a deciduous tree, and seems to be thriving in Philippine forests. The wealth of the forests seems almost inexhaustible, but the Philippines also suffers great forest destruction—through illegal cutting, typhoons, floods, and other damage. Reafforestation is highly favoured in capital allocation. The aims of reafforestation are to develop a forest cover on all open lands—as a protection for water courses as well as a source of revenue. A great deal of money, effort, and research are going into the development of the Philippine natural resources.

OVERSEA TRADE:

The Philippines is constantly looking for new oversea markets, and is anxious to expand trade with Australia, whose vast natural resources go largely to the Japanese market. Australia exports milk products, coke, coal, and Australian-assembled cars to the Philippines, but trade is largely one-sided—very little is exported from the Philippines to Australia. This seems to be the trend with most of the Philippines' oversea trade-agreements. Unilateral agreements exist between Australia and the Republic reducing import tariff on Philippine handicrafts and other goods, but the present lack of trade balance will probably continue for some time, because both countries grow sugar, pineapples, copra and timber.

Zebu-cross cattle

Finance for development: The main source of finance for Philippine development comes from taxes, and the present budget requires over two billion pesos, received through internal revenue and customs duties. The Government realizes that the vast resources of the Philippines will require a tremendous expenditure for full development. This will have to come not only from Government finance and private enterprise within the Philippines but also from oversea resources. Recently a legislation called the Investment Incentives Act was passed, stating in clear and specific terms the conditions under which foreign investment may be made. These conditions favour foreign investors, and point out the various attractions of investment in various enterprises. The Government guarantees repatriation of capital, remittance of profits, and certain incentives to assist growth of assets over a period of years. Legislation has been passed and approved by President Marcos exempting machinery and equipment needed by a foreign investor from customs duty, provided it is used in certain areas defined by law.

The principal trading partner of the Philippines is the United States; there is a 45% reciprocal import-export trade between these two countries. The next largest trading partner is Japan. Many products are being developed to appeal to the Australian market, apart from furniture and hemp, which are already exported to Australia in large quantities. Raw wool can be exported from Australia to be woven in the Philippines, and the finished product imported—some of the cloths are of superlative quality. In the future there is likely to be a greater trade between the Philippines and other countries.

Developing exports: The Philippines is experimenting with a number of new export possibilities, and developing others on a much larger scale. Pulp could be a very important export, possibly rivalling that of Canada, and another promising product is Philippines marble, of various colours, already proved to be an excellent decorative building material. Mining has also increased, though the Philippines still relies on oil imported from Indonesia and the Middle East for 91% of its industrial energy. In all, 15 metallic, and 25 non-metallic minerals are mined in the Philippines, including gold, silver, platinum, copper, lead, nickel, manganese, zinc, chromium, and mercury—and among non-metals, cement, gypsum, and marble.

Another promising export is shell. Before the Spaniards came, the Filipinos used shells as currency, as did other peoples of the Indo-Pacific. When the Spaniards came, they were impressed by the many shell ornaments, and noticed that the windows of many Filipino houses were also made of shell.

In the 19th century, a shell lampshade industry was born, with Kapiz shells. These shells are also used for buttons, ornamental table mats, wall panelling, and are even made into chandeliers and tables. The Kapiz is only found in waters surrounding the Philippines. A full-grown shell is only about a sixteenth of an inch thick, and fishermen gather the shells from the coral reefs at low tide. The meat is taken out, and eaten—it is regarded as a delicacy—and the shells are put on ants' nests to be picked thoroughly clean by the insects. The shells are then sorted—there is a difference between the shells of male and female shellfish. The sorted shells are treated with acid to loosen the outer coating, then scraped and brushed. After this they are soaked in water and dried, before finally being laminated and shaped into whatever object is required.

Fishermen sell these shells by the thousand, at prices ranging from U.S.$3.50 to U.S.$4.50.

Some of the most beautiful exports of the Philippines are hand-embroidered materials. The expert fingers of the Filipino women sew and weave many

94

patterns on various types of cloth. The popular locally-made fabrics—piña, from pineapple fibres, ramie, from a type of grass, jusi, called "thai silk", and abaca cloth, made from a kind of banana fibre—have many uses. They can be made into dresses, handbags, household articles such as table mats and napkins, tablecloths, curtains and upholstery, and into fine shirts for men.

Perhaps the most beautiful of these fabrics is piña. This was first used as a cloth in the 18th century. Weaving the cloth from pineapple fibre is one of the oldest crafts in the Republic. Piña was exhibited in London 200 years ago, and attracted widespread European interest; but owing to the large amount of work involved in its production at that time, it was not considered for export.

Ramie, another versatile fabric, is made from a grass which usually fares best on volcanic soil. The best fibres come from grass actually growing on the slopes of volcanoes. The grass grows rapidly, reaching a height between five and seven feet within two or three months. It is called the "wonder grass", because it can be harvested four times a year. The tensile strength of Ramie is eight times that of cotton.

Jusi, made from fibres grown in the Visayas, is similar to piña. It is sent to Japan or China for processing, and comes back to the Philippines for final work such as weaving and embroidering. Jusi is spun with synthetic fibres to make the popular fabric called "thai silk".

Abaca is a comparatively new cloth, though the same fibres have always been a main export as Manila hemp. The fibres used for dress materials are very fine, and take about two weeks to weave into a piece of fabric 11 yards long and 20 inches wide. This material has a natural off-white colour, but it can be dyed. The cloth is processed in varying grades, from quite coarse fabric to a very fine weave.

Embroidering of any of these locally-made fabrics takes about three months for a gown made to order, but plenty of stores sell and export such clothing "off the hook".

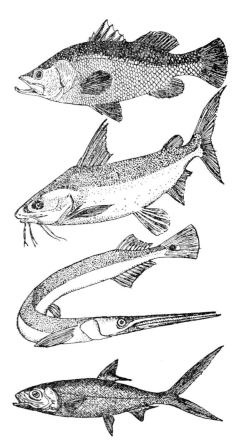

Commercial food fishes—from top, Giant Perch, Salmon Catfish, Long Tom, Salmon Herring (The herring, called Bangos by the Filipinos, is farmed in tidal pools)

PLACES TO SEE

The variety of life and scenery of the Philippines offers a great deal to any traveller. The Filipino people, an oriental mixture of Hindus, Arabs, Persians, and Malays, is for the most part friendly, hospitable, generous, and well educated. Though Filipinos speak about 87 dialects, and Tagalog is the national language, English is taught in all schools and spoken and understood everywhere. Spanish also is spoken fluently in parts of the land.

There are many ways to see a country—I had my recent visit planned; this way you travel in comfort and see all there is to see in the time available to you. I flew in with QANTAS, and within the islands my journeying was arranged by Benny Farolan, of Sita World Travel, in Manila.

AROUND MANILA

Manila city, with its crowded streets and market places, has much for the visitor to see—the colourful transport and heavy traffic, with its incessant horn-blowing; the sweepstake ticket sellers and cigarette pedlars; the art galleries, historic buildings and quiet parks, the Palace, the modern buildings of Makati, and the Escolta or main shopping centre; the central market where produce is brought for sale each day, and the market people, busily bargaining for articles on display from dried fish to balut.

Manila has ample accommodation. I stayed at the Hotel Filipinas, which I can recommend to anyone. The tariff, U.S.$8.00 a day, is very reasonable—the rooms are air-conditioned and self-contained, with television and radio. Meals are extra, but a really good meal can be had from $1.20 to $3.00. Other hotels provide just as good accommodation, including the newly-built ones on Roxas Boulevard, but their tariffs may be dearer.

Bleeding-heart Pigeon

COLOUR
Sunset over Manila Bay
Doing the laundry in the traditional manner
Growing rice is a family concern
A farm house in Mindanao

96

The National Museum: In the National Museum you can trace the history of man in the Philippine area, through stone tools and primitive axes, ancient pottery, and other artifacts. Carbon testing has shown that man was living in this part of the world at least 22,000 years ago. Clay pottery in the museum dates back to 700 B.C.—the pots were probably used for cooking rice.

Some of the pottery is definitely Chinese, probably traded between the 7th and 17th centuries. The Chinese merchants brought fine porcelain to trade for Philippine goods and, as such pottery could not be made in the islands, it became a prized possession—so valuable that when a person died porcelain wares were buried with the body. The more wealthy the person, the more porcelain goods were buried with him.

Intramuros: This walled city is the scene of the original capital at Manila, built 50 years after the Spanish discovery of the Philippines. Now a ruin, it was once a well-planned city, with cobbled lanes, streets and plazas, and tiled-roofed houses. Outside the city's high walls flowed a moat, in the old European style of protection. Fort Santiago, within the walled city, the dreaded prison used by the Spaniards and later by the Japanese, is today kept in spotless condition and is open to visitors. At one end is a museum housing the relics and personal effects of Jose Rizal, national hero of the Philippines.

Cemeteries of interest: In the heart of Manila lies the Paco Cemetery—resting place of the victims of a cholera epidemic in 1820. The arched niches in its old, mossy, circular walls are now empty and covered with trailing ivy; the cemetery is no longer used for burials. Today it is a quiet, pleasant park, with centuries-old trees and old-world garden, where many visitors come seeking a change from the noisy streets of the city.

A short distance away, in the suburbs of Manila, is the colourful Chinese Cemetery, with its elaborate and colourful pagodas, linked by paved roads, and, at one end, a Chinese temple.

Near the area of Forbes Park is Fort McKinley, and the United States Military Cemetery. Here lie buried the remains of 17,177 United States World War II dead. Neat rows of white crosses, white buildings, shady trees and green lawns give a feeling of peace and serenity. The cemetery is situated in the grounds of the barracks for the Army of the Philippines.

Mouse Deer, or Chevrotain

San Agustin Church: This church, within the walled city of Intramuros, is the oldest building in the Philippines. First built of nipa palm and bamboo, in 1571, it was destroyed by the Chinese pirate Limahong during a raid in 1574. A second building, of wood, replaced it in 1583. Later, in 1599, the present building was begun. This has adobe walls, with beautifully carved ceilings and columns, and imported European chandeliers. It was completed in 1601. The pulpit, a work of art, and the wooden seats in the choir loft are intricately hand-carved. In the vestry, with its long hall and high roof, the Spaniards officially handed over the Philippines to America. This building seems to be the only earthquake-proof structure in the islands. In the passageways at the side of the church hang old paintings, some still bearing the marks of bullets.

Inside the church stands the tomb of the founder of Manila, Legazpi. The church was bombed, machine-gunned and shelled during World War II, but withstood the damage, though the convent beside the church was destroyed.

101

Malacañang Palace: The official residence of the President of the Philippines, Malacañang Palace stands on the banks of the Pasig River. The street outside the Palace is called Jose P. Laurel, after the president who lived there during the Japanese Occupation. Leading from the street, between huge wrought-iron gates, is a neat driveway which takes visitors to the Palace itself. The grounds were originally the estate of a Spanish Grandee, and later became the home of the Spanish governors, then the American Governor-General, and now the presidents of the Republic. The name "Malacañang" comes from a Tagalog phrase "may lakan diyan", meaning "there are noblemen living here".

Ferdinand Marcos, President of the Philippines

Entering the Palace, you pass through a porch and up broad stairs of Philippine mahogany. The stairway and reception room are laid with carpet, and beautiful chandeliers hang from the Palace ceilings. When these are lit, thousands of prisms reflect light, giving sparkling colours of many hues. Inside are many magnificent rooms, such as the First Lady's reception room, and the main dining room with its carved chairs and long table made from the trunk of one mahogany tree. You may move out onto a balcony, overlooking the river, where small boats ply to and fro. Across the river lies Malacañang Estate, containing administrative dwellings for the palace guards and officers. Each bank has little jetties, for the use of the boats.

In the Palace Grounds stand more administrative offices, a radio station and television station, orchid houses, garden plots, and, under the old trees, statues telling of the old Philippines.

Santo Tomas University: In 1605, when Spaniards had been in the Philippines for 40 years, a school of higher learning was envisaged by Father Miguel de Benavides, the Archbishop of Manila. The Archbishop died that year, but his idea had been adopted by the Dominicans. Donations were received, including money left by the Archbishop in his will. King Philip III of Spain doubted the useful purpose of a university in Manila, but in 1609, permission to build was given, and foundations begun in 1611. The college was officially recognized in 1619, and in 1624 King Philip IV allowed it to confer degrees. Pope Innocent X promoted the college to the rank of university in 1645, with the right to confer degrees in Arts, Philosophy, and Theology. It opened its faculty of Medicine and Pharmacy in 1871, and of Dentistry in 1904.

The museum at Santo Tomas contains an art gallery, with old masterpieces. This museum began operation in 1682. The university also has the oldest library in the Philippines, with a rich collection of rare books, printed from the 15th century onwards, including classical literature from all nations. The University Press, founded in 1593, is the oldest printing firm in the Republic. The university is open to visitors.

Corregidor: One of the most famous islands of the Philippines is a two-and-three-quarter square mile islet of rock and jungle at the entrance to Manila Bay, called Corregidor. The name comes from the Spanish "corregir" meaning "to correct", for in the days of the Spaniards they used this small island as a check-point and guardian of Manila Bay and the city itself. All ships had to stop at Corregidor to have their papers checked before going on to Manila.

The Filipinos and Americans made their famous stand against the Japanese invaders here in World War II. Today it is a National Shrine, where people can see the Malinta Tunnel, headquarters of General MacArthur and General Wainwright, the mile-long barracks used by the soldiers, and the guns left there after the siege. You fly across to the island from Manila, or go by hydrofoil—a 45-minute trip.

Matabungkay Beach: Two hours' drive from Manila lies Matabungkay Beach, in Batangas province. Its blue water, white sand, and refreshing surf are ideal for the traveller who wants a quiet day's relaxation, swimming, fishing, or skin-diving. Nipa palm huts and sheds, providing cool shelter, can be rented for the day or longer, and meals can also be bought here.

Tagaytay and Lake Taal: The city of Tagaytay, 45 miles from Manila and 2,250 feet above sea level, overlooks volcanic Lake Taal—the "lake on an island on a lake on an island". Next to the lookout is a restaurant and hotel, so visitors are well catered-for. On the way to Tagaytay you pass coconut plantations used mainly for copra production. On some, workers collect the hearts of the palms for the manufacture of palm wine. The journey also takes you through fishing grounds, rice-growing areas, orchards, and old country towns.

Las Piñas bamboo organ: The Las Piñas Church, visited by many travellers on their way to Tagaytay, is famous for its magnificent bamboo organ. Construction of this instrument began in 1818, and took three years to complete. Each of the 950 pieces of bamboo used had to be covered in sand for six months after cutting, to preserve the wood from the bamboo bug. To the right of the church entrance stands a little shop selling curios, at some of the cheapest prices in Manila. The shop is run by Sister Helen, a Canadian who speaks a number of languages, and who teaches at the school next door.

Pagsanjan Falls: About an hour and a half's drive south-east of Manila you find the Pagsanjan Falls. On the way, you pass an inland body of water called Laguna de Bay, and the Los Banos Agricultural College before coming to the small town of Pagsanjan. From here, boats take travellers up the river to Pagsanjan Falls. The river passes through deep gorges, and the boats slide by many small waterfalls before reaching the main falls, cascading through a rainbow mist. On the way back, the boats "shoot the rapids", plunging through turbulent water and dodging huge boulders, steered by their expert boatmen, until they reach the more placid waters of the main river.

NORTHERN LUZON

From Manila north to Baguio, the summer capital of the Philippines, you travel about 180 miles. Philippine Airways can take you there in about 40 minutes, for a return fare of about U.S.$8.00, or you can go by road or rail. A trip by road takes about four hours, and the railway journey takes a little under six hours.

Baguio, on a 5,000 foot high plateau, has a refreshing climate and beautiful scenery, with parks, gardens, the President's summer mansion, the Country Club, the United States Army's recreational centre, Camp John Hay,

103

*Pigmy negrito from
the mountains of
Northern Luzon*

and the Philippine Military Academy. The parks and gardens were laid out by one of the best American landscape architects. Baguio is the home of the Igorots—the world-renowned woodcarvers.

Baguio has three hotels, and average charges, without meals, range from U.S.$5.00 to $7.00 for single accommodation, and from U.S.$7.00 to $9.00 for double rooms.

Banawe Rice Terraces: These spectacular terraces were built 3,000 years ago by the Ifugaos. The mountain ranges have been chiselled into a vast series of "stairs" leading up the sides of the mountains. The individual terraces, from two to over eight feet high, combine to rise 5,000 feet. Among the terraces, little houses, built of local materials, can be seen.

Accommodation at Banawe varies from U.S.$2.00 to $2.50. To reach Banawe from Manila, you travel by car with an overnight stop at Bontoc, the capital of the mountain province. The rice paddies are about 30 miles from this town. Bontoc has two hotels, with accommodation costing from U.S.$2.00 to $6.00.

La Union: Less than two hours' drive from Baguio lie the beach resorts of La Union, with water skiing, fishing, boating, and swimming. You can hire a beach cottage or stay in a hotel. Costs, without meals, vary from U.S.$3.00 to $10.00, and a meal will cost between U.S.60 cents and $1.50.

Hundred Islands National Park: This is recognized as the second biggest marine park in the world. It has underground caves, coral gardens, white sandy beaches, and warm, clear water. The park actually includes over a thousand small islands, dotted about the Lingayen Gulf, and is five hours' drive from Manila, or you can reach it in much shorter time from Baguio. Accommodation costs from U.S.$2.00 to $5.00.

SOUTHERN LUZON

Legaspi, nearly 350 miles from Manila, in the province of Albay, Southern Luzon, an area of natural splendour, with lakes, mountain peaks, and the mighty Mayon Volcano, can be reached by rail or air. The journey by rail takes about eleven and a half hours, and costs U.S.$4.00 return fare. By air, you reach Legaspi in one and a half hours, for a return fare of U.S.$13.00.

There are many hotels in Southern Luzon. The best of these range in price from U.S.$4.00 for single accommodation to $5.00 double accommodation, without meals.

SOUTHERN
LUZON

Mount Mayon: A perfect cone that rises 8,000 feet above sea level, Mount Mayon is the most famous natural monument in Southern Luzon. The best time to see the volcano is in the early morning, before clouds come down to hide it. Mount Mayon's most destructive eruption occurred in 1814, when it buried the town of Cagsawa. You can still see the tops of houses and the church steeple rising from the lava that covered the town many years ago. Except for the ruins, no one could guess what had happened, for green grass now covers the spot, and people still live round the volcano. A rest house has been built half way up the side of the mountain, and farmers cultivate the slopes and rich soil at the base of the slumbering giant.

104

The boiling lakes: In the town of Tiwi, one of Mount Mayon's air-holes has been harnessed—in the form of thermal baths and private pools. From Tiwi you can see the boiling lakes—holes like large cauldrons, filled with boiling water.

Abaca factory: In Southern Luzon, centre of Philippine abaca industry, you can visit the plantations, and see the stripping of fibres and final treatment of the famous Manila hemp. Other products can be made from abaca fibres—table mats, baskets, handbags, abaca cloth for clothing, and many things useful in homes throughout the world.

THE SOUTHERN ISLANDS

This part of the Philippines—the Visayas, Mindanao, and the Sulu Archipelago—has comparatively few visitors. You can travel to Zamboanga, in Mindanao, and on to the island of Jolo, by Philippine Airways, stopping en route in Cebu City and Davao. The first-class fare is U.S.$54.00 return—very reasonable for a trip of over 1,000 miles.

The southern islands of the Philippines have about 13 hotels, ranging in price from U.S.$4.00 to $6.00 for single accommodation, and from U.S.$5.00 to $11.00 for double rooms. This price does not include meals, which cost between U.S.70 cents and $1.50. A service fee is charged by all the hotels—usually 10% of the total price paid for rooms and meals.

Cebu City: At Cebu, the oldest city in the Philippines, on the island of Cebu in the Visayas, Magellan in 1521 erected a cross, now called the Cross of Magellan. This cross is housed in a tiled-roof building near the waterfront, open to visitors. A statue of the patron saint of the island, the Holy Child of Cebu, stands in San Agustin Church. From Cebu City, the busiest city in the islands outside of Manila, the traveller can branch out to anywhere in the Visayas.

Mactan Island: This island, off the middle of Cebu's east coast, has a wealth of history. In the town of Opon stands a monument to Magellan, and also a monument to Lapu-Lapu, the warrior who killed him.

Bacolod: Bacolod City, on the northern end of Negros Island, the nearest western neighbour of Cebu, has become the centre for the main sugar-growing area of the Philippines. Nearby rises Kanlaon volcano, which last erupted at the beginning of this century. For those who like music, Bacolod has the only symphony orchestra outside of Manila. Not far from the city lies a beach area, with good swimming.

Iloilo: Another attractive island, with a busy seaport; from Iloilo come the famous fabrics called piña and jusi. Clothes such as dresses for the Filipino women and barong tagalog, the beautifully locally-made shirts, are manufactured on Iloilo, and can be bought much cheaper here than in Manila.

Mindanao: Farther south lies the second largest island in the Philippines, Mindanao—abaca and pineapple-growing country. One of the best hotels in the islands can be found at Davao, Mindanao's largest city. The penal colony at Davao contains experimental farms, an orchid-breeding plantation, gardens, and parks. Davao has many shopping centres, with many Chinese stores. A few miles to the south-west of Davao stands Mount Apo, commonly known as the "Chief". Round the base of this 9,610-foot-high mountain spreads a national park, with waterfalls and hot springs. Osmeña Park has been made into a botanical and zoological garden, famous for its orchids, as well as many other kinds of plants.

Lake Lanao: This lake, 2,300 feet above sea level, has become a home of the Muslim people of Mindanao. Here you can buy Muslim handicrafts—silks and brassware. Marawi City is rich in history, legends and beauty, but for the best brassware the visitor usually has to go to Macadaw, a few miles from Marawi.

Some of the many kinds of orchids grown in the Philippines

Zamboanga City: The capital city of Mindanao, Zamboanga stands on the south-eastern tip of the island, a centre for the Muslim people, and not far from Sandakan in North Borneo. This is a main port for smugglers from Sandakan. Naval vessels patrol near the harbour by day, to prevent smugglers entering the busy port; but the smugglers have many other places on the coast to land. They use long boats of hollow tree trunks, fitted with five high-powered outboard motors. The faster these craft travel, the more they plane, and fast naval boats find themselves hard-pressed to get anywhere near them when the outboards use full-power.

In Zamboanga City stand the houses of the Muslim people, with their colourful outrigger boats, called vintas, anchored out in the water. At night the Muslims use these vintas to catch fish, aided by powerful lights, while others silently glide along the foreshore, in front of the Bayot hotel, trying to sell sea shells, pearls, and anything else they can induce foreign travellers to buy.

To Zamboanga the "sea-gypsies" travel from Borneo and Indonesia, spending all their lives on board their boats on the seas between the islands.

The language spoken in many parts of Zamboanga City is closer to Spanish than any other language in the Philippines. Some class it as a patoi; people are addressed as "Señor", "Señorita", and "Señora", and public notices are printed in Spanish-style language.

In Zamboanga, a light-hearted, small, friendly city, shopping is pleasant with no rush. You can wander round the city itself, or along the waterfront among the market stalls. Muslim brassware, silks, and other goods can be bought very cheaply if you have the time and patience to bargain. Pedlars, selling synthetic diamonds, rubies and emeralds, cultured pearls and baroque pearls (those with an irregular shape) can be found everywhere, but particularly round the hotels.

I found Zamboanga City one of the most colourful and interesting places in the Philippines, with a leisurely way of life, and clean, warm, sunny climate.

106

TO VISIT THE PHILIPPINES...

The increase in visitors to the Philippines has been about 20% each year since 1951. The annual influx of oversea visitors exceeds 80,000—most from America, but large numbers also from Japan, and the rest from Australia or Europe. QANTAS and other airlines can take you to the Philippines from any part of the world. From Sydney the journey takes seven hours' flying time, through Darwin, Port Moresby or Djakarta, or direct. From Europe, the Philippines is 17 hours' flying time, and from the west coast of America, 15 hours. From Japan, the trip takes three hours. Shipping lines also call at Manila.

Entry formalities: To enter the Philippines you should have a valid passport and a current visa, easily obtainable at any Philippines consulate in the world. You can stay in the Philippines for 72 hours without a visa, but no cost is involved in getting one, and it is wise to have it. Visa fees have been abolished for nationals of Australia, the United States, Belgium, Denmark, Germany, Bolivia, Indonesia, Italy, Japan, Korea, Luxembourg, Netherlands, New Zealand, Norway, Spain, Sweden, Thailand, and Tunisia. The maximum length of time allowed for a visit is 59 days. Multiple visas are required for visitors travelling in a party, and multiple entry-visas are needed if a traveller intends to call at the Philippines, visit another country, and return to the Philippines.

Currency: Any amount of foreign currency can be brought into the Philippines, and exchange centres are situated in the International Airport and at the Docks. Visitors are advised to cash money only at banks or with the cashier of their hotel; counterfeiters operate from time to time. The U.S. dollar is worth about three pesos 89 centavos, but sometimes this rises to four pesos. The Philippines is one of the least expensive places in the world to visit.

Customs formalities and duty-free imports: The traveller is met with courtesy and co-operation by the customs officers, and usually is not submitted to baggage inspection. Pretty girls from the Philippines Tourist and Travel Association greet travellers with flowers, and help them through customs, also giving them any information they may want. Travellers to the Philippines are allowed to bring in 300 cigarettes, one quart of spirits, 50 cigars or two pounds of pipe tobacco, and any number of cameras and film provided they are for the traveller's own use.

Health requirements: Current vaccinations for smallpox and cholera are necessary. Visitors without these are held at the airport or at the docks until

107

the injections are given. The Philippines is a member nation of the World Health Organization.

Climate and clothing for visitors: The Philippine climate is tropical, with two seasons—the wet, from late June to early November, and the dry, from late November to early May. The gayest months are April and June, when most of the fiestas are held.

Clothing should be light and washable. In the mountains of Baguio, 5,000 feet above sea level, you may need a coat or pullover. Most Filipino men wear the barong tagalog—a finely woven shirt of pineapple fibre, worn outside the trousers. The women wear beautifully embroidered frocks of light cloth. At official functions men usually wear a coat and tie or a barong tagalog, which is acceptable on any occasion. Laundry and dry-cleaning are available, with either normal or rapid (take away in the morning and return by the same evening) service.

Transport: The public bus fare, within the city limits, is 20 centavos for a one way trip. Jeepneys (converted jeeps) carry eight or ten passengers, sitting along each side of the covered vehicle. These jeepneys are gaily coloured and spectacularly ornamented, often carrying amusing slogans such as "My love will wait". You can see these jeeps being converted at the factory, alongside the road to Tagaytay.

Taxi cabs are plentiful, charging 15 centavos for flagfall and the first 250 metres, and five centavos for every 250 metres after. With thousands of cars and other vehicles on the roads, I saw surprisingly few accidents. The expert way Filipinos handle their vehicles is extraordinary, but slightly unnerving for passengers. Public transport is often in short supply in Manila, and students coming home from university at night may wait up to an hour for buses.

Other means of transport can be the converted motor scooter with side car, or the slow, quaint horse-drawn calesa, with its driver, the "cochero". These conveyances are attractively ornamented with silver.

If you want to take a private hire car, arrange the cost of the journey with the driver beforehand. Do not engage the vehicle until you have agreed on the fare. The usual price for the car and driver is about 10 pesos an hour.

Philippine Airways fly to all parts of the islands, and have all kinds of aircraft, including the lastest prop-jet Hawker Siddeley 748S—the most comfortable prop-jet plane I have travelled in. Other airlines also run inter-island services, and the Philippine National Railway serves Luzon and other islands. Diesel-electric locomotives pull freight cars and first-class, air-conditioned passenger cars, imported from Japan. Coastal shipping plies between Manila and all Philippine ports.

Shopping: Souvenirs and other items can be bought from street pedlars or any of a wide variety of shops throughout the islands, but the cheapest and most reliable places to buy are in the markets, in every city. Like most Eastern shopkeepers, Filipinos love to bargain for an article, so do not accept the first price quoted. A shopkeeper showed me a gold watch for 280 pesos; when he saw the shock on my face, he came down to 130 pesos, and we started bargaining from there, with great enjoyment.

Filipinos in national dress

108

The Banawe rice terraces in the Mountain Province, said to be 3,000 years old

A rice stack, after the harvest

*Abaca, ready for shipment, to be made
into Manila hemp*

The grapefruit seller skins the fruit
you buy

Fish is plentiful, and prices are cheap
in the coastal districts of Mindanao

Selling cockerels at Zamboanga

Roadside sellers of fruit, in Zambo-
anga, Mindanao

The bird seller outside Manila Cathedral on a Sunday morning

COLOUR
Mosque in a village in Mindanao
Vintas are colourful as well as practical
Muslim girl from Mindanao
Bamboo poles are used for the
Tinikling, a vigorous Filipino dance

*Part of the Chinese Cemetery outside
Manila*

All kinds of transport can be hired in the Philippines

QUEZON CITY

MANILA

Pasig R.

San Juan R.

The provinces

— city border
▪▪▪ railway
--- main road

	Government
	Cemetery
	Commerce
	Industry & transport
	Recreation & housing

Ilocos Norte
Abra
Ilocos Sur
La Union
Mountain Province
Cagayan
Isabela
Nueva Viscaya
Pangasinan
Zambales
Nueva Ecija
Tarlac
Pampangan
Bulacan
Bataan
Manila Rizal
Cavite Laguna
Batangas
Camarines Norte
Camarines Sur
Catanduanes
Marinduque
Albay
Sorsogon
Mindoro Occidental
Mindoro Oriental
Romblon
Masbate
Samar
Antique Capiz
Iloilo
Aklan
Northern Leyte
Palawan
Negros Occidental
Cebu
Negros Oriental
Bohol
Southern Leyte
Surigao del Norte
Misamis Oriental
Surigao del Sur
Zamboanga del Norte
Zamboanga del Sur
Misamis Occidental
Lanao del Norte
Lanao del Sur
Bukidnon
Agusan
Davao
Sulu
Cotabato

(MALAYSIA)

Batan Is

Babuyan
Is

LUZON

The islands

Mindoro

THE
VISAYAS

Samar

Panay

Leyte

Cebu

Palawan

Bohol

Negros

MINDANAO

Sulu
Archipelago

N

Index